Kid's Box

New Generation

British English

Caroline Nixon &
Michael Tomlinson

Activity Book
with Digital Pack

Thanks and Acknowledgements

Authors' thanks

Many thanks to everyone at Cambridge University Press & Assessment for their dedication and hard work, and in particular to:

Louise Wood for doing such a great job overseeing the level; Catriona Brownlee for her dedication and sound editorial judgement; freelance editor Melissa Bryant.

We would also like to thank all our pupils and colleagues, past, present and future, at Star English academy in Murcia, especially Jim Kelly for his friendship and support throughout the years.

Dedications

For Jim Kelly: Here's to the next thirty years of our Starship enterprise. – CN

To my Murcian family: Adolfo and Isabel, the Peinado sisters and their other halves for always treating me so well, thanks for being there and for making my life in Murcia so much fun. – MT

Illustrations

Ana Sebastian (Bright Agency); David Belmont, Javier Joaquin, Laszlo Veres, Moreno Chiacchiera (Beehive); Shahab (Sylvie Poggio Artists).

Audio

Audio production by Sounds Like Mike Ltd.

Design and typeset

Blooberry Design.

Additional authors

Rebecca Legros and Robin Thompson (CLIL); Montse Watkin (Sounds and life skills)

The authors and publishers acknowledge the following sources of copyright material and are grateful for the permissions granted. While every effort has been made, it has not always been possible to identify the sources of all the material used, or to trace all copyright holders. If any omissions are brought to our notice, we will be happy to include the appropriate acknowledgments on reprinting and in the next update to the digital edition, as applicable.

Key: U = Unit, V= Values

Photography

The following photos are sourced from Getty Images:

U0: Ableimages/DigitalVision; FatCamera/E+; Monty Rakusen/Image Source; Compassionate Eye Foundation/Martin Barraud/Stone; teekid/E+; mediaphotos/iStock/Getty Images Plus; Tom Werner/DigitalVision; John Harper/The Image Bank Unreleased; Hanna Hruts/iStock/Getty Images Plus; Tatyana Soloshenko/iStock/Getty Images Plus; photosynthesis/iStock/Getty Images Plus; Anna Erastova/iStock/Getty Images Plus; **U1:** metamorworks/iStock/Getty Images Plus; all images copyright of Jamie Lamb - elusive-images.co.uk/Moment; simonkr/E+; Tony Garcia/Image Source; Dmytro Aksonov/E+; Nettiya Nithascharukul/EyeEm; nndanko/iStock/Getty Images Plus; Thanapol Kuptanisakorn/EyeEm; Tracy Ducasse/Moment; Jacky Parker Photography/Moment; FARBAI/iStock/Getty Images Plus; Sudowoodo/iStock/Getty Images Plus; MicrovOne/iStock/Getty Images Plus; Aleksandra Alekseeva/iStock/Getty Images Plus; Vitalii Barida/iStock/Getty Images Plus; **U2:** Maskot; triloks/iStock/Getty Images Plus; Ben_Gingell/iStock/Getty Images Plus; SDI Productions/iStock/Getty Images Plus; Riska/E+; JGI/Jamie Grill/Tetra images; CasarsaGuru/E+; skynesher/E+; Thomas Northcut/DigitalVision; kali9/E+; Cavan Images; Westend61; adoc-photos/Corbis Historical; filmstudio/E+; Yellow Dog Productions/The Image Bank; David Madison/Stone; Marc Romanelli/Tetra images; Andrii Shablovskyi/iStock/Getty Images Plus; abadonian/iStock/Getty Images Plus; izusek/E+; Richard Drury/DigitalVision; miodrag ignjatovic/E+; tomazl/E+; Yulia_Artemova/iStock/Getty Images Plus; Bubanga/iStock/Getty Images Plus; succodesign/iStock/Getty Images Plus; PeterSnow/iStock/Getty Images Plus; **U3:** Michael Blann/DigitalVision; Tomas Rodriguez/Stone; Nikada/E+; cglade/iStock/Getty Images Plus; By Eve Livesey/Moment; guvendemir/E+; Kypros/Moment; JGI/Tom Grill/Tetra images; ZoltanGabor/iStock/Getty Images Plus; Copyright Artem Vorobiev/Moment Open; R.M. Nunes/iStock/Getty Images Plus; ollegN/iStock/Getty Images Plus; Sensvector/iStock/Getty Images Plus; veronawinner/iStock/Getty Images Plus; **U4:** George Diebold/Photodisc; Haje Jan Kamps/EyeEm; John Parrot/Stocktrek Images; Historical/Corbis Historical; Juanmonino/E+; Westend61; shannonstent/E+; Ascent/PKS Media Inc./Stone; Gary Yeowell/DigitalVision; traumlichtfabrik/Moment; George Pachantouris/Moment; paul gadd/The Image Bank; Carl & Ann Purcell/Corbis Documentary; Salvatore Virzi/EyeEm; Phathn Sakdi Skul Phanthu/EyeEm; artpartner-images/The Image Bank; reklamlar/iStock/Getty Images Plus; samxmeg/E+; Dorling Kindersley; Matt Mawson/Moment; Jeremy Woodhouse/Photodisc; **U5:** Pulse/Corbis; Petra Schüller/iStock/Getty Images Plus; OlegSam/iStock/Getty Images Plus; LinaTruman/iStock/Getty Images Plus; posteriori/E+; lilkar/iStock/Getty Images Plus; Metkalova/iStock/Getty Images Plus; cocodava/iStock/Getty Images Plus; frantic00/iStock/Getty Images Plus; Kyle Monk/Tetra images; piyaphat50/iStock/Getty Images Plus; chameleonseye/iStock/Getty Images Plus; Tatsuo115/iStock/Getty Images Plus; benedek/E+; Marina Inoue/Moment; Daniel_M/iStock/Getty Images Plus; Rajanish Kakade/AP; Blake Callahan/Moment; Jamroen Jaiman/EyeEm; Yoonjung Park/EyeEm; Deborah Cardinal/Moment Open; margouillatphotos/iStock/Getty Images Plus; StockFood/Foodcollection; Anna Blazhuk/Moment; Corbis/VCG; Dennis Welsh/UpperCut Images; Donald Iain Smith/Stone; John Howard/The Image Bank; View Pictures/Universal Images Group; ksana-gribakina/iStock/Getty Images Plus; **U6:** Caia Image/Collection Mix: Subjects; Klaus Vedfelt/DigitalVision; Marc Dufresne/iStock/Getty Images Plus; monstArrr_/iStock/Getty Images Plus; Zia Soleil/Stone; Robert Daly/OJO Images; Viktorcvetkovic/E+; GlobalP/iStock/Getty Images Plus; eli_asenova/E+; yusufsarlar/E+; vasileva/iStock/Getty Images Plus; bergamont/iStock/Getty Images Plus; luba/E+; Creative Crop/Photodisc; RedHelga/E+; Phill Thornton/iStock/Getty Images Plus; Pawel_B/iStock/Getty Images Plus; DustyPixel/E+; Wivoca/iStock/Getty Images Plus; choness/iStock/Getty Images Plus; TokenPhoto/E+; Thanee Chooha Noom/EyeEm; Easy_Asa/iStock/Getty Images Plus; IvanSpasic/iStock/Getty Images Plus; Mayur Kakade/Moment; Rob Van Petten/Photodisc; Francesco Riccardo Iacomino/Moment; Amarita/iStock/Getty Images Plus; KuznetsovDmitry/iStock/Getty Images Plus; Floortje/E+; courtneyk/iStock/Getty Images Plus; FG Trade/E+; Obaba/iStock/Getty Images Plus; Prostock-Studio/iStock/Getty Images Plus; Nikiteev_Konstantin/iStock/Getty Images Plus; Color_life/iStock/Getty Images Plus; peri priatna/iStock/Getty Images Plus; senkoumelnik/iStock/Getty Images Plus; owattaphotos/iStock/Getty Images Plus; **U7:** fizkes/iStock/Getty Images Plus; EcoPic/iStock/Getty Images Plus; Picture by Tambako the Jaguar/Moment; Steve Satushek/The Image Bank; Rawlinson_Photography/E+; miflippo/iStock/Getty Images Plus; Ian Peter Morton/iStock/Getty Images Plus; gremlin/E+; Byrdyak/iStock/Getty Images Plus; Denja1/iStock/Getty Images Plus; Christian Sanchez/500px Prime; mauricallari/iStock/Getty Images Plus; Jose Luis Pelaez Inc/DigitalVision; WOLFGANG KUMM/DPA; doomko/iStock/Getty Images Plus; prahprah/iStock/Getty Images Plus; Yulia Zelinskaya/iStock/Getty Images Plus; Jasius/Moment; **U8:** LanaStock/iStock/Getty Images Plus; Vesnaandjic/E+; DeanDrobot/iStock/Getty Images Plus; PeopleImages/iStock/Getty Images Plus; shishir_bansal/iStock/Getty Images Plus; Ascent Xmedia/Stone; Zero Creatives/Image Source; Maxian/E+; Barry Austin/DigitalVision; Nancy Honey/Photodisc; Peathegee Inc/Tetra images; Image Source/Stockbyte; Prostock-Studio/iStock/Getty Images Plus; mbbirdy/E+; pyotr021/iStock/Getty Images Plus; Imgorthand/E+; Cavan Images; Janie Airey/Image Source; SDI Productions/E+; Spiritartist/E+; JulyVelchev/iStock/Getty Images Plus; artisteer/iStock/Getty Images Plus; motimeiri/iStock/Getty Images Plus; Arra Vais/iStock/Getty Images Plus; VladislavStarozhilov/iStock/Getty Images Plus; eli_asenova/E+; shapecharge/E+; Maskot/DigitalVision; fstop123/E+; tatyana_tomsickova/iStock/Getty Images Plus; Westend61; Pacharada17/iStock/Getty Images Plus; Natariis/iStock/Getty Images Plus; **V12:** Marisvector/iStock/Getty Images Plus; **V34:** Halfdark/fStop; **V56:** mikkelwilliam/iStock/Getty Images Plus.

The following photos are sourced from other libraries:

U1: Pictorial Press Ltd/Alamy Stock Photo; **U7:** Matthijs Kuijpers/Alamy Stock Photo.

Cover Photography by Tiffany Mumford for Creative Listening.

Commissioned photography by Stephen Noble and Duncan Yeldham for Creative Listening.

Contents

Welcome to our blog

 1 Put the words in groups.

book

scarf

program

| book comic |
| costume internet |
| magazine newspaper |
| program scarf |
| screen sweater |
| trainers Wi-Fi |

 2 Match the sentences with Stella, Lenny and Meera.

1 I had a good holiday.

2 I'd like to write about sport.

3 I didn't see you online.

4 I'm ready for a new school year.

5 I'm sending you the information now.

6 There's a competition for the best blog in the school.

 ▢ ▢

 ▢ ▢

 1 ▢

 3 Read and complete.

| blog ~~diary~~ internet music |
| online photos sports videos |

A blog is a kind of (1) _____diary_____ which you write (2) _____. You can do a search and find one on the (3) _____. You can read about football, tennis and other (4) _____. You can get information about technology and the world around us. You can look at lots of really interesting (5) _____, listen to all your favourite (6) _____ and watch different kinds of (7) _____. Lenny, Stella and Meera write the new **Kid's Box** (8) _____. They want to win the school blog competition. There's a great prize!

 4 Correct the sentences.

1 A blog is a kind of book.
No, it isn't. It's a kind of diary.

2 You can find blogs in the shops.
_____
_____

3 **Kid's Go** is a new blog.
_____
_____

4 The three writers are called Fahad, Lola and Li Jing.
_____
_____

5 There's a prize for the worst blog.
_____
_____

Language: present simple questions and short answers

▯ Do the online activities on **Practice Extra** as you complete this unit

1 Read and order the text.

	blog for young people. There are
	are Meera, Lenny and
9	Meera likes the natural world and drawing. She
	don't have to go to school.
	things. Lenny likes computers and sport, Stella
5	Stella. They all go to the same
	three writers. Their names
1	**Kid's Box** is an exciting new
	school: City School. They all like different
	really loves taking photos, too. They write
	likes singing and music, and
	their blog at the weekend when they

2 Read and complete the questions.

How many   What   ~~What's~~
When   Where   Why

1 _____What's_____ the blog called?

It's called **Kid's Box**.

2 _____ _____ writers are there?

There are three.

3 _____'s the blog about?

It's about the things that they like.

4 _____ do they write the blog?

They write it at the weekend.

5 _____ do they write it then?

They write it then because they don't have to go to school.

6 _____ can you see the blog?

You can see it on the internet.

3 Write the correct sentences.

~~Stella would like~~	oldest of	a village.
Stella	to school	~~singing and music.~~
Meera walks	are both	Lenny.
Lenny's the	lives near	the children.
Meera	~~to write about~~	ten.
Stella and Meera	lives in	every day.

1 Stella would like to write about singing and music.

2 _____

3 _____

4 _____

5 _____

6 _____

Choose words from the box to label the pictures.

dictionary   exam   geography   history   language   maths   music   ~~science~~

science _____   _____   _____   _____   _____   _____

 Follow the school words.

classroom	sea	back	beans	cave	eagle	rice
geography — history	potatoes	mountain	music	teacher	board
beard	maths	English	knee	sport	lake	subject
salad	river	computer studies	tortoise	art	soup	ears
moustache	yoghurt	exam	dictionary	science	elbow	field

 Now complete the table with words from Activity 2.

The body	Food	The natural world
elbow		

Two words are 'odd'? What are they? _____

Which group are they from? _____

 Answer the questions.

1 What's your school called?   My school's called _____

2 What's your favourite subject?   _____

3 What was your first subject yesterday? _____

4 Do you have lunch at school or at home? _____

5 What did you do after lunch yesterday?   _____

6 Did you have any homework yesterday?

1 Read and complete the school timetable.

- Quinn does these subjects at school: geography, history, music, maths, English, sport, computer studies, art, science.
- English is his last class on Mondays.
- His favourite day is Wednesday. He has sport at ten o'clock and music at eleven o'clock. He also has geography in the morning.
- On Thursdays his history class finishes at four o'clock and he has English at eleven o'clock.
- On Mondays he studies a lot. Before lunch he has maths after science and at eleven o'clock he has computer studies. After lunch he first has geography and then he has history.

- Maths is his last class on Tuesdays and Wednesdays.
- After science on Friday, Quinn does these subjects in alphabetical order: history, sport, computer studies, music, English.
- The first class on Mondays and Fridays is the second class on Tuesdays.
- On Tuesdays the first class is computer studies. Before lunch he has geography and at two o'clock he has sport.
- He always has art after lunch, but not on Mondays or Fridays.
- He has music after art on Thursdays.
- He has science four times a week.

	Monday	Tuesday	Wednesday	Thursday	Friday
9.00–10.00				maths	science
10.00–11.00					
11.00–12.00					
lunch					
13.00–14.00					
14.00–15.00			English		
15.00–16.00					

 2 Now write about Quinn's timetable on Monday.

On Monday _____

_____

_____

 3 Write about your timetable on your favourite school day.

My favourite school day is _____

_____

_____

Sounds and life skills
Chatting with friends

Pronunciation focus

1 🎧 2 **Listen and circle the connected words.**

1 Hi. (How are) you?

2 How was your summer?

3 Are you happy to be back?

4 How about you?

5 Did you have fun?

2 🎧 3 **Listen and complete.**

Hi. (1) ___How___ ___are___ things?

Good thanks. (2) _____ you?

I'm fine, thanks. (3) _____ have a good summer?

It was great! We went to the beach for a holiday. How about you? (4) _____ do anything fun?

I went to football camp. It was amazing! (5) _____ happy to be back?

Yes, it's nice to see everyone.

3 **Read and match.**

1 What did you do for your holidays?

2 Did you go swimming?

3 Who did you go with?

4 How long did you stay there?

5 Was the weather nice?

a My family.

b We were there for a week.

c Yes, it was sunny every day.

d I went to the beach.

e Yes, I did. The sea was lovely.

4 **Look at the picture of your friend. Write questions to ask him about his holiday.**

_____

_____

_____

_____

1 Read and answer.

1 Who's older: Sir Doug or Diggory Bones? Sir Doug is older than Diggory.
2 How long is the model dinosaur? _____
3 What are Diggory's students learning about? _____
4 What did The Rosetta Stone help us to do? _____
5 Where was Diggory's computer? _____

2 Read the text. Then look at the code and write the secret message.

Egyptian hieroglyphics were one of the first kinds of writing, but modern people couldn't understand them. Ancient people wrote important things on The Rosetta Stone in three different languages.

In 1822 a very clever man called Jean-François Champollion used two of the languages to understand the third, the Egyptian hieroglyphics. The Rosetta Stone helped us to understand the past better.

a	b	c	d	e	f	g	h	i	j	k	l	m
n	o	p	q	r	s	t	u	v	w	x	y	z

V e r y _____ .

_____ .

_____ .

Do you remember?

1 An internet diary is called a _____ blog _____ .

2 The children want to write a blog for their school _____ .

3 We use a _____ to find the meaning of words.

4 _____ is the school subject about different places in the world.

5 At school we learn about plants and the human body in _____ .

Can do

I can talk about school subjects.

I can ask my friends about their school timetable.

I can write about my favourite school day.

Remember to complete the online activities for this unit on Practice Extra

Time for television

What's the time?

It's six o'clock.

(six) o'clock

five to (seven)

ten to (seven)

quarter to (seven)

twenty to (seven)

twenty-five to (seven)

half past (six)

five past (six)

ten past (six)

quarter past (six)

twenty past (six)

twenty-five past (six)

to | past

1 Match the clocks with the times.

1 ten to four

2 ten past four

3 five to four

4 quarter past four

5 twenty-five past seven

6 twenty past four

2 Look and write the times.

five past
eleven

_____   _____   _____   _____   _____

3 Read and draw the times on the clocks.

1 David wakes up at 7.10 on Mondays, Wednesdays and Fridays.

2 Nick leaves home at 8.55 in the morning.

3 Alex sometimes plays football at 15.30.

4 Anna always starts her homework at 16.00.

5 Akash watches his favourite programme on TV at 18.45 on Tuesdays and Thursdays.

6 Petra goes to bed at 21.00 every night.

Do the online activities on Practice Extra as you complete this unit

1 Match the clocks with the sentences for William's day yesterday.
Put the sentences in order.

a He had lunch at half past twelve. _____

b Classes started again at quarter to two. _____

c He caught a bus to school at twenty-five past eight. _____

d School finished at four o'clock. _____

e William caught the bus home at ten past four. _____

f William got dressed at ten to eight. __1__

g He went out to the playground for break at quarter to eleven. _____

h Classes began at nine o'clock. _____

2 Find the past of these verbs and write them.

w	a	g	o	t	u	p	u
o	e	y	p	l	k	e	d
k	o	n	u	s	c	j	r
e	i	q	t	o	o	k	a
u	o	p	a	s	y	l	n
p	c	a	u	g	h	t	k
k	b	d	t	i	c	a	f
h	c	a	m	e	h	o	d

go   went

come   _____

have   _____

catch   _____

wake up   _____

get up   _____

eat   _____

drink   _____

put   _____

take   _____

3 Answer the questions about yesterday.

1 What time did you get up?
   I got up at _____

2 What time did you go to school?
   _____

3 Where did you have lunch?
   _____

4 What time did you go home?
   _____

5 What did you eat for dinner?
   _____

6 What did you drink in the evening?
   _____

4 Now write 20–30 words about what you did yesterday.

Yesterday, I

1 Choose words from the box to label the pictures.

cartoon   comedy   documentary   news   quiz   series   sport   ~~weather~~

1 ___weather___   2 _____   3 _____   4 _____   5 _____   6 _____

2 Write the programmes.

1 On this you can see swimming, basketball, tennis or motorbike racing. ___sport___

2 This programme's funny, with funny people. _____

3 We watch this programme to see if it's hot or cold today. _____

4 This is on every day. It's about important things around the world. _____

5 A programme which tells us interesting facts about animals, history or places. _____

6 This programme has episodes and can be on TV every day. _____

3 Read and answer the questions.

Channel 1	Channel 2	Channel 3	Channel 4
12.10 Fun house (cartoon) 1.00 The news 1.45 The weather 2.15 Chelsea v Milan (football) 4.15 Animals of Africa (documentary)	11.50 Top songs (music videos) 12.30 Friendly (comedy) 2.10 Count to ten (quiz) 3.15 Giants v Bouncers (basketball)	12.30 The news 1.05 Explorers (documentary) 1.45 The weather 2.20 Annie (musical comedy film) 3.45 Cartoon hour	1.15 Maskman returns (film) 2.30 Our body (documentary) 3.15 Answer first (quiz) 3.55 Laugh out loud (comedy)

1 What time is the news on Channel 3? At 12.30.

2 What channels are the cartoons on? _____

3 What's on Channel 1 at quarter to two? _____

4 What are the names of the two quiz programmes? _____

5 What are the documentaries about? (1) _____ , (2) _____ , (3) _____

6 What time is the film on Channel 4? _____

1 Read and complete the table.

Now it's four o'clock. Four friends have got a problem because they can't decide which programme to watch.

- Sophia's favourite programme starts in 20 minutes and is called **Quacky Duck**. She likes cartoons, but doesn't like documentaries or sports programmes.

- The other girl, Petra, loves quiz programmes.

- **Who wants to be a billionaire?** started at 3.50.

- Frank loves playing sport and he likes watching it too. His favourite programme starts in 45 minutes.

- The other boy's favourite programme is called **World about us**. He's the only child who likes documentaries.

- The documentary starts at ten past four and the cartoon starts at twenty past four.

- Deniz doesn't want to watch **Sunday sports**.

- Finally they all decide to watch Petra's favourite programme, but it started ten minutes ago!

Name	Sophia			
Kind of programme				
Programme name	Quacky Duck			
Programme time				

2 Now answer the questions.

1 Who doesn't like documentaries? _Sophia, Petra and Frank_

2 What's the name of the programme they decide to watch? _____

3 When did it start? _____

4 Whose favourite programme is it? _____

5 Who doesn't want to watch what's on TV at 4.45? _____

6 When does the cartoon start? _____

3 Answer the questions.

1 What's your favourite TV programme?

My favourite TV programme is _____

2 What kind of programme is it?

_____

3 What time is it on?

_____

4 How many words can you find in 'documentaries'?

star, mice, _____

_____

_____

_____

_____

Sounds and life skills
Deciding together
Pronunciation focus

1 🎧 **4** **Listen and write 1 and 2.**

a [2] sheep [1] cheap

b [ ] share [ ] chair   d [ ] ships [ ] chips

c [ ] shoes [ ] choose   e [ ] washes [ ] watches

2 🎧 **5** **Choose words from Activity 1. Listen and check.**

1 The farmer bought _____cheap_____ _____sheep_____ .

2 The students had to _____ a _____ .

3 I have to _____ some new red _____ .

4 The sailors always eat fish and _____ on the _____ .

5 Charlie _____ the children as she _____ her hands with soap.

3 🎧 **6** **Read and write. Listen and check.**

Can't you watch the race on your phone?   OK. I'll watch **Sing Up!** on catch up later.
~~Ooh. Sing Up! is on in ten minutes.~~   Perfect!

Shannon: Ooh. Sing Up! is on in ten minutes.

Chuck: Oh! But I wanted to watch the Formula 1 race!

Shannon: _____

Chuck: Let me check … Yes, I can!

Shannon: _____

Chuck: Yes, but it's more exciting to watch on the big TV screen!

Shannon: _____

4 **Read and complete the TV questionnaire.**

1 _____How_____ _____many_____ **hours** of TV do you watch every week?

I watch ten hours every week.

2 _____ do you usually watch TV?

I usually watch TV around eight o'clock.

3 _____ do you watch TV?

I watch TV on the sofa in my living room.

4 _____ ever watch TV before school?

No, I don't. I don't have time!

1 Read and answer.

Diggory Bones

1 What's The Baloney Stone? <u>It's a computer program of old languages.</u>
2 Where's The Baloney Stone? _____
3 What time did Emily turn on the TV? _____
4 Which programme did Diggory want to watch? _____
5 Who was the cameraman at the university? _____
6 What does Brutus Grabbe want? _____

2 Read the story so far and then write it in the past.

The story so far ...
Diggory's in a classroom at the university. The reporter and the cameraman arrive. The reporter asks Diggory some questions. Diggory says that he doesn't want the thief to use The Baloney Stone to find treasure. At half past nine Diggory asks Emily to turn on the TV because he wants to watch the news. Brutus Grabbe comes onto the TV screen and laughs. He's the TV cameraman from the university! He wants Diggory's secret password for the computer program.

The story so far ...
Diggory was in a classroom at the university.
_____
_____
_____
_____
_____
_____
_____

Do you remember?

1 The time in words is quarter to eleven. The time in numbers is _____10.45_____.
2 The time in numbers is 8.25. The time in words is _____.
3 A _____ is a TV programme which tells us interesting things about our world.
4 Two TV programmes which usually make us laugh are _____ and _____.
5 Two words with 'sh' (as in '<u>sh</u>ow') are _____ and _____.
6 Two words with 'ch' (as in '<u>ch</u>annel') are _____ and _____.

Can do

I can tell the time in English.

I can talk about different kinds of TV programmes.

I can write about my favourite TV programme.

How can we make nature documentaries?

1 **Read and circle the adjectives.**

Last week I watched a (great) documentary called **Nature at Home**. It's about all the animals and insects that live in people's gardens. You can watch it on **DiscoveryPix**. I found it really interesting because there were a lot of insects in one place at one time. I loved watching the butterflies. They're so beautiful and colourful. The photography in the documentary is amazing. I know you enjoy nature programmes, so you must watch it.

2 **Plan to write a chat message. Complete the information about a documentary.**

13:02   56% 🔋

What did you watch?   Yesterday I watched _____ .

What's it about?   It's about _____ .

Where can you watch it?   You can watch it on _____ .

What was it about?   Last night's episode was about _____ .

What did you like about it? I found it _____ because _____ .

Why do people enjoy watching it?   People enjoy watching it because _____ .

3 **Use your notes to write a message to a partner about the documentary.**

4 **Did you ...**

- ☐ plan your message?
- ☐ use adjectives to make it more interesting?
- ☐ read your message again?
- ☐ check grammar, spelling and punctuation?

Writing tip

We use adjectives to describe things. You can use adjectives in your writing to make it more interesting.

You must watch it because you can learn about **interesting** animals. The photography is **beautiful** too!

Flyers Listening Part 5

1 🎧 7 **Listen and colour and write. There is one example.**

2 People at work

We use *going to* to talk and write about the future.

Affirmative	Negative (n't = not)	Question
I'm **going to be** a nurse.	He **isn't going to be** a dentist.	**Is** he **going to be** an actor?
She's **going to visit** me.	We **aren't going to do** it.	**Are** they **going to clean** it?

 1 **Write the words in the sentences.**   be   listen   play   read   ~~watch~~   wear

1 She's going to ____watch____ TV after school.

2 He's going to _____ a fire fighter when he's older.

3 They aren't going to _____ a comic.

4 We're going to _____ to pop music.

5 I'm going to _____ my new trainers.

6 You aren't going to _____ badminton today.

2 **Match the questions with the answers.**

1 How are you going to find the street? [e]

2 What time's he going to get up? [ ]

3 Where are we going to have lunch? [ ]

4 Who are they going to talk to? [ ]

5 Which T-shirt are you going to wear? [ ]

6 Why's he going to go to the music festival? [ ]

7 When's she going to play basketball? [ ]

8 What are they going to do after school? [ ]

a They're going to talk to their friends.

b I'm going to wear my blue one.

c We're going to have it at home.

d He's going to listen to rock music.

e We're going to look at a map.

f He's going to get up at half past seven.

g They're going to do their homework.

h She's going to play on Saturday.

 3 **Look at this code. Write the secret message.**

	1	2	3	4	5
1	a	b	c	d	e
2	f	g	h	i	j
3	k	l	m	n	o
4	p	q	r	s	t
5	u	v	w	x	y

a = 11, b = 21, c = 31

11–34–51   55–53–15   22–53–42–43–22   54–53   31–53–33–51
A r e   _____   _____   _____   _____

54–53   33–55   14–11–34–54–55?
_____   _____   _____?

 4 **Now write another message for your partner in your notebook.**

Do the online activities on Practice Extra as you complete this unit

1 Look at the pictures and answer the questions.

1 What are they going to do?   They're going to wash their clothes.
2 What's she going to do?
3 What's he going to do?
4 What are they going to do?
5 What's he going to do?
6 What's she going to do?

2 Look and make negative sentences.

1 He isn't going to catch the bus.   4
2   5
3   6

3 Look at Tanaz's diary for the weekend. Ask and answer the questions.

Friday	morning	School
	afternoon	4 pm Play football
Saturday	morning	10.45 Visit Grandma
	afternoon	2 pm Shopping for pyjamas
Sunday	morning	Walk in hills
	afternoon	4 pm Cinema

1 a Where / Tanaz / go / Friday morning
     Where's Tanaz going to go on
     Friday morning?
  b She's going to go to school.

2 a What / Tanaz / do / Friday afternoon

  b

3 a What time / Tanaz / visit her grandma

  b

4 a What / Tanaz / buy / Saturday afternoon

  b

5 a Where / Tanaz / walk / Sunday morning

  b

6 a What / Tanaz / do / Sunday afternoon

  b

Choose words from the box to label the pictures.

actor   cook   dancer   designer
football player   journalist   mechanic   ~~pilot~~

pilot   _____   _____

_____   _____   _____

 Complete the table.

person	verb
teacher	teach
	drive
dancer	
	skate
	design
run	
	photograph
manager	
tennis player	
	swim

 Read and write the words in the puzzle.

1 Someone who drives buses.
   A bus driver _____.

2 Someone who works with food.
   A _____.

3 Someone who stops fires.
   A _____.

4 Someone who looks after our teeth.
   A _____.

5 Someone who works in a hospital.
   A _____.

6 Someone who flies planes.
   A _____.

7 Someone who repairs cars.
   A _____.

8 Someone who paints pictures.
   An _____.

9 Someone who acts in films.
   An _____.

```
      1  b  u  s  d  r  i  v  e  r
                 2
   3                
               4    
               5    
      6            
   7              
      8            
         9         
                 ↑
```

What's the mystery job? _____

Now write a definition for this job.

_____

_____

_____

1 These four children are going to have different jobs. Write the numbers.

 a
 b
 c
 d

a ☐ ☐ ☐   b ☐ ☐ ☐   c 1 ☐ ☐   d ☐ ☐ ☐

1 He's going to fly planes.
2 He's going to travel a lot.
3 He's going to repair cars.
4 She's going to use eggs.
5 He's going to get dirty.
6 She's going to wear a white hat.

7 He's going to visit lots of airports.
8 She's going to work in a kitchen.
9 She's going to look after people's teeth.
10 He's going to work with machines.
11 She's going to tell children not to eat sweets.
12 She's going to wear gloves and a mask.

2 Slim Jim's a famous singer. Read and complete his diary.

- He's going to meet his manager after lunch on Friday.
- The same day that he sings, he's going to open a new school in the morning.
- He's going to go to the cinema next Thursday afternoon.
- After lunch on the day he arrives in London, he's going to talk to some children who are in hospital.
- He's going to have a TV interview before lunch on the day he goes to the cinema.

- He arrives at London airport next Monday morning.
- On the same day that he's having dinner with some actors, he's going to visit a music shop in the morning.
- He's going to sing in a big football stadium.
- He's flying to Spain on the morning of the same day that he's going to meet his manager.
- He's going to have dinner with some actors next Tuesday evening.

	Monday	Tuesday	Wednesday	Thursday	Friday
a.m.					
	lunch	lunch	lunch	lunch	lunch
p.m.					meet manager

3 Answer the questions.

1 Where are you going to go after school this afternoon? I'm going to go _____

2 Who are you going to see this evening? _____

3 When are you going to do your homework? _____

4 What time are you going to go to bed tonight? _____

Sounds and life skills
Thinking about the future
Pronunciation focus

 8 **Listen and circle the /ə/ sounds. Then practise saying the sentences.**

1 (I)'m going (to) be (a) teach(er).
2 She wants to be a driver.

3 Maybe I can be a pop singer.
4 What are you going to be?

 9 **Listen and complete.**

Emma

I think I'm going to be a ___writer___
when I'm _____.
I love cooking for _____.
Maybe I can be a food _____.

Oliver

I think I'm going to be a _____.
Maybe I can be your food _____.
Maybe sometimes I can be a
_____ in your restaurant.

 Read and match.

1 Must love children. Must be creative and good at speaking English.   a an actor
2 Must love animals. Must be good at driving a tractor.   b a farmer
3 Must be a good communicator. Must love people and food.   c a fire fighter
4 Must not be scared in front of a lot of people. Must be good at   d a waiter
  remembering words.   e an English teacher
5 Must be brave. Must be good at climbing.

 How are jobs similar and different? Read and complete.

> cars   creative   look after
> ~~outside~~   restaurant   stage

> actor   cook   dentist
> driver   ~~farmer~~   writer

1 farmer, fire fighter, police officer
   They all usually work (_outside_), but
   only a (_farmer_) looks after animals.

2 driver, engineer, mechanic
   They all love (_____), but only a
   (_____) drives one.

3 cook, manager, waiter
   They all work with food in a (_____),
   but only a (_____) makes it.

4 painter, photographer, writer
   They're all (_____), but only a
   (_____) uses words.

5 dentist, doctor, nurse
   They all (_____) you, but only a
   (_____) looks at your teeth.

6 actor, dancer, singer
   They all like to work on a (_____),
   but an (_____) doesn't need music.

1 Read and answer.

Diggory Bones

1 What's Diggory's job? <u>He's an archaeologist.</u>
2 Where does Brutus want Diggory to meet him? _____
3 Why did Diggory call him 'a pirate'? _____
4 What time are Diggory and Emily going to meet Brutus? _____
5 Is Brutus at the library? _____
6 Who's got a letter for Diggory? _____

2 Read and order the text.

has got the program, but he wants Diggory's ☐

ancient languages. Brutus Grabbe took it from ☐

The Baloney Stone is a very important computer ☐1

secret password. Brutus went on the evening news ☐

at the Old City Library at 10.45, but Brutus wasn't there. ☐

on TV to speak to Diggory. He told him to meet him ☐

program which can help us to understand ☐

Diggory's classroom at the university. Now Brutus ☐

Do you remember?

1 A ___pilot___ flies planes.
2 A mechanic _____ cars.
3 When people have problems with their teeth, they see a _____ .
4 We use '_____ _____' to talk and write about the future.
5 Two words that end in the /ə/ sound (as in 'doct<u>or</u>') are _____ and _____ .
6 Two jobs that don't end in the /ə/ sound (as in 'nurse') are _____ and _____ .

Can do

I can use *going to* to talk about the future.

I can talk about people at work.

I can write about different jobs.

How can we stay safe?

 1 **Read and match.**

SAFETY ON THE ROADS

It's important to stay safe on the roads, especially when riding a bike. Here are some safety tips:

1 Always wear
2 Make sure you use hand
3 Always ride
4 It's important to keep your bike
5 Always look out for

a signals when you slow down or turn a corner.
b in good condition.
c with lights at night.
d other vehicles on the roads.
e a helmet in case you have an accident.

FOLLOW THIS ADVICE AND STAY SAFE! — — —

2 **Plan to write a safety leaflet. Complete the information about staying safe online.**

Staying Safe Online

Dos

It's important to _____ .
Always _____ .
_____
_____
_____
_____

Don'ts

Don't _____ .
Never _____ .
_____
_____
_____
_____

 3 **Use your notes to create a leaflet about staying safe online.**

 4 **Did you ...**
- ☐ plan your leaflet?
- ☐ use imperatives?
- ☐ read your leaflet again?
- ☐ check grammar, spelling and punctuation?

Writing tip

We use imperatives when it's important to do something. You can use imperatives with **always** and **never** to show something is very important in your safety leaflet.

Always wear a helmet.

Never play with fire.

Social science: safety procedures | 🛡 critical thinking

1 **Read the letter and write the missing words. Write one word on each line.**

Dear KBTV,

Last Saturday I saw something on your channel about a new quiz show

Example for young people. It's _____called_____ **Boxing Clever.**

I wrote to you last year about a different programme, but you needed

1 people who were older _____ me. I think this new quiz show is

2 for children of my age, and we have to _____ questions about

3 different school subjects. I'm very _____ at geography and

history, but science is my best subject.

4 I would like _____ go on the quiz show. Please can you send

5 me _____ more information so that I can show my parents?

From

Li Wei

1 **Read the story. Choose words from the box to complete the sentences.**

> channel   documentary   fire fighter   going
> history   jobs   painted   ~~programme~~   quiz   time

FRIENDLY

Friendly is a really funny comedy (1) _____programme_____ . It's on TV at twenty to five every day. In this show there are five friends who all go to the same school in a big city. They live and study in the school, but they aren't all in the same class.

They're all going to have different (2) _____ when they grow up. Peter wants to be a cook, Jenny wants to be an actor, Sally wants to be a taxi driver, Jim wants to be a (3) _____ and Frankie wants to be an artist.

In the story last week, Frankie (4) _____ a picture for an art competition and Jenny sat as a model for her. In the picture which Frankie painted, Jenny had one square eye, which was red, and a carrot for a nose. One of her legs was a mobile phone and the other was a banana. Frankie's friends don't think she's (5) _____ to win the competition, but Frankie's happy. She knows she isn't going to be a famous artist!

2 **Choose a title for this episode of Friendly.**

a   Modern art
b   Fun and games
c   Beautiful people

3 **Draw and colour Frankie's painting.**

4 **Match the questions with the answers.**

1   Why do zebras like old films?
2   What goes up slowly and comes down quickly?
3   What's a chicken's most important test at school?
4   What do you call bears with no ears?
5   What's always slow to come, but never arrives?
6   When do elephants have eight feet?

- [ ] An eggzam!
- [ ] When there are two of them!
- [ ] B.
- [1] Because they're in black and white.
- [ ] An elephant in a lift!
- [ ] Tomorrow.

5 Complete the sentences. Count and write the letters.

1 The winner of the competition gets a
   _____prize_____ .   [5]

2 The study of the past is called
   _____ .   ☐

3 Eight fifteen is _____
   past eight.   ☐

4 We draw and paint in this lesson.
   _____   ☐

5 Good, better, _____ .   ☐

6 The study of different countries
   is called _____ .   ☐

7 A competition with questions is a
   _____ .   ☐

8 Somebody who repairs cars is a
   _____ .   ☐

9 Something we study at school is called
   a _____ .   ☐

10 A manager works on this in an office.
   A _____ .   ☐

11 Eleven thirty is _____
   past eleven.   ☐

12 The study of numbers is called
   _____ .   ☐

13 Somebody who paints pictures is
   an _____ .   ☐

14 The opposite of work is _____ . ☐

6 Now complete the crossword. Write the message.

p | r | i | z | ²e

Message row 1: | 1 | 2 | 3 | 3 | 4 | | 5 | 1 | 2 | 6 | 2 |
| | e | | | | | | | | e | | e |

7 Quiz time!

1 What languages can they study at City School? They can study _____
_____

2 In which lesson do we learn about plants and the human body?
_____

3 How can we film animals from the air?
_____

4 What does Stella think she's going to be?
_____

5 What jobs did George Orwell have?
_____

6 What can we use to cover flames in a fire? _____

8 Write questions for your quiz in your notebook.

City life

right ↱ left ↰ straight on ⇑ corner ↰ past □↑ across ⇷ along ⇐

 Read and answer the questions.

Yesterday afternoon five people got on a bus at the bus station: one man, two women and two children. The bus left the station at nine o'clock. It had to stop at the corner because the traffic lights were red. The bus turned left after the traffic lights.

The bus didn't stop at the first bus stop, but drove straight on because there weren't any people waiting there and no one wanted to get off. The bus turned right at the next corner and drove over the bridge. At the second bus stop, outside the school, the two children and the man got off and nine more people got on. Then the bus went into the train station, where ten people got off and 12 more got on. The bus drove out of the station, turned left and went straight on to the end of the road.

1 How many people got off at the second stop?

_____

2 How many times did the bus turn left?

_____

3 How many people were there on the bus when it drove out of the train station?

_____

 Tick (✓) or cross (✗) the sentences.

1 Yesterday morning six people got on at the bus station: two men, one woman and three children. _____

2 The bus had to stop at the corner because the traffic lights were red. _____

3 After the first bus stop, it turned left at the next corner. _____

4 At the second bus stop, outside the hospital, the two children and the man got off. _____

Read and complete the sentences.

~~across~~   along   left
on the corner   right   straight on

1 She ran _____across_____ the park.

2 She turned _____ at the corner of Queen Street.

3 He went _____ at the traffic lights.

4 He waited for his friend _____ outside the school.

5 She turned _____ into King Street.

6 He walked _____ Prince Street.

28   **Language:** directions and prepositions   ▶ Do the online activities on Practice Extra as you complete this unit

1 Follow the directions and write the message.

London	to	29	places	million	is
of	see	the	interesting	in	and
lots	are	year	visit	people	every
biggest	There	UK.	it.	city	the

r = right   l = left   u = up   d = down

London – 5r – 3d – 5l – 4r – 2u – 2l – 2d – 1l – 1u – 1l – 1u – 3r – 1u – 2l – 1d – 4r – 1d – 3l – 2u – 2r – 2d – 1l – 1d

London _____ is _____ the _____ _____ _____ _____

_____ _____ _____ _____ _____ _____

_____ _____ _____ _____ _____ _____

_____ _____ _____ _____ _____ _____

2 Put these buildings on the map.

1 The gym's on the right of the supermarket.
2 The cinema's opposite the bus station.
3 The castle's opposite the car park.
4 The library's between the café and the toyshop.
5 The school's on the other side of the road from the bookshop and opposite the hospital.
6 The bookshop's behind the fire station.
7 The stadium's on the other side of the road from the bookshop, on the corner.

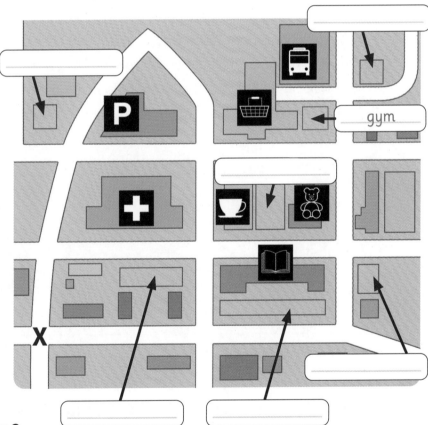

3 Find these buildings in Activity 2.

1 Start at the X. Go straight on and take the first road on the right. Go past the hospital and the café. It's the building on the left before the toy shop. What is it? _____

2 Start at the X. Turn right and walk to the fire station. Go past the fire station and walk to the next corner. Turn left. It's on the corner on the right. What is it? _____

4 Now write two sets of directions for a partner to follow in your notebook.

Look and complete the words.

1 h o t e l   3 th _ _ t _ _   5 c _ _ _ _ l _

2 r _ _ t _ _ r _ _ t   4 p _ l _ _ _ _ st _ t _ _ _   6 a _ _ p _ _ _ _

 Complete the table. Look in the Pupil's Book to find the names of the places.

Yesterday Yuna visited London with her family.

- At nine o'clock Yuna went to a place where you can see exciting things from all over the world.
- They went for a boat trip on the River Thames at half past ten.
- After lunch they went to the place where Shakespeare and his actors showed their plays.
- They took a taxi from Tower Bridge at half past five and went back to their hotel.
- They had a picnic lunch at quarter to one. They ate some sandwiches in Hyde Park.
- After visiting the theatre, they went to look at an old building next to Tower Bridge.
- They arrived at their hotel at ten to six. They had dinner and went to bed.

9.00	Went to the British Museum.
10.30	
2.30	
4.30	
5.50	

 Look at the letters on the clock and write the words.

1 It's five to one.   straight

2 It's eight o'clock.   _____

3 It's ten to six.   _____

4 It's ten past nine.   _____

5 It's twenty-five past four. _____

6 It's twenty-five to three. _____

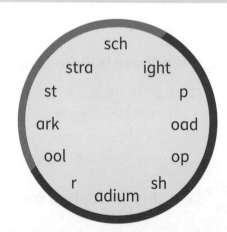

1 Write 'who', 'which' or 'where'.

1 A place _____where_____ you can post letters and postcards.

2 Someone _____ flies planes.

3 Something _____ you have to buy when you go by bus or train.

4 A place _____ we go to see a play.

5 Someone _____ cooks food in a restaurant.

6 A place _____ you can see old paintings and books.

7 A place _____ you can catch a plane.

8 A place _____ you can get money.

9 Someone _____ repairs cars.

10 A place _____ you go to cross a river.

2 Now find the words from Activity 1.

a	c	e	t	u	r	e	d	p	m
i	q	p	i	l	o	t	b	m	u
r	c	y	c	s	z	a	r	e	s
p	o	s	t	o	f	f	i	c	e
o	b	p	h	d	o	v	d	h	u
r	a	a	e	u	l	k	g	a	m
t	n	k	a	o	a	n	e	n	y
c	k	w	t	k	r	o	t	i	p
f	t	b	r	t	p	i	e	c	o
s	u	c	e	t	i	c	k	e	t

3 Write a definition of these words.

1 A place _____
_____
_____
_____

2 Someone _____
_____
_____
_____

4 Put these places on your map.

airport   bank   ~~castle~~   hotel
museum   restaurant   theatre

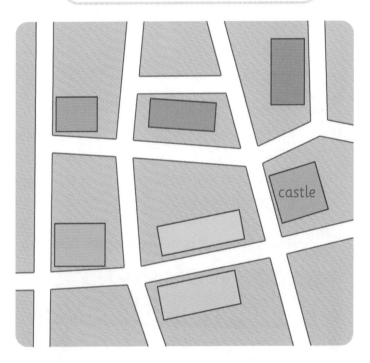

5 Now write directions from the castle to three places on the map.

1 Start at the castle. Go ...
_____

6 Ask your partner to follow your directions.

Sounds and life skills
Choosing options
Pronunciation focus

 10 Match to make words. Listen and check.

1	st	-orts stadium
2	str	-ool
3	sp	-ore
4	sky	-are
5	sch	-scraper
6	squ	-eet

 **11 Listen and circle.**

1 What time does the
sports stadium / (swimming pool) open?
2 Why don't we visit the museum at the top of the
skyscraper / store?
3 Look at the map and go straight on up the
stairs / street.
4 You don't have to **stand / study** at the
school / sports stadium.
5 Let's go **skating / skateboarding** along that
stream / street.

 12 Listen and match.

1 The British Museum
2 Tower Bridge
3 A boat on the river
4 The London Eye

a is a special way to travel in a big city.
b is exciting and fun, with amazing views.
c is a great place to take photos.
d has lots of interesting things to see inside.

 Read the poster. Then write about a place to visit in your town or city.

Come and visit
The Tower of London.

It's an amazing and interesting castle.
You can see the Queen's crowns and necklaces inside.
It's next to the Thames River and Tower Bridge.
The easiest way to get there is by metro or river boat.

Come and visit _____

It's _____ .

You can see _____ .

It's next to _____ .

The easiest way to get there is _____

_____

1 Read and answer.

Diggory Bones

1 Why was it the wrong library? <u>Because it was the wrong city.</u>
2 Which city does Brutus mean? _____
3 What are they going to do now? _____
4 What is there outside Alexandria? _____
5 What's on the walls of the cave? _____
6 Who's the taxi driver? _____

2 Who said it? Read and match.

 1    2    3    4

a I think he means the city of Alexandria in Egypt. | 1

b Brutus can use The Baloney Stone to understand the writing! ☐

c What are we going to do now? ☐

d … can open the door to mountains of secret treasure! ☐

e Now let's get a taxi and find a hotel. ☐

f Yes, son. ☐

Do you remember?

1 An actor often works in a _____theatre_____ .
2 You can stay in a _____ when you go on holiday.
3 Be careful when you walk _____ the road. Look out for cars!
4 The opposite of 'turn right' is 'turn _____'.
5 Two words with a 'st' (as in '<u>st</u>ation') are _____ and _____ .
6 Two words with a 'sp' (as in '<u>sp</u>orts') are _____ and _____ .

Can do

I can talk about places around town.

I can give and understand directions.

I can write directions to places around town.

What are the best modes of transport?

1 **Read and circle.**

Quick and Easy Transport

One of the **more good** / (**best**) ways to travel around the busy cities of Vietnam is by rickshaw. You can travel **faster** / **fastest** than by taxi this way, and the rickshaw is also the **more** / **most** eco-friendly way to travel these days. It doesn't need fuel, so it's **better** / **best** for the environment than cars. Rickshaws are bicycles with a seat in the front for passengers. The driver sits behind. It can only take one or two passengers, but it's definitely **quicker** / **quickest** than a taxi!

2 **Plan to write an advert. Complete the information about a mode of transport.**

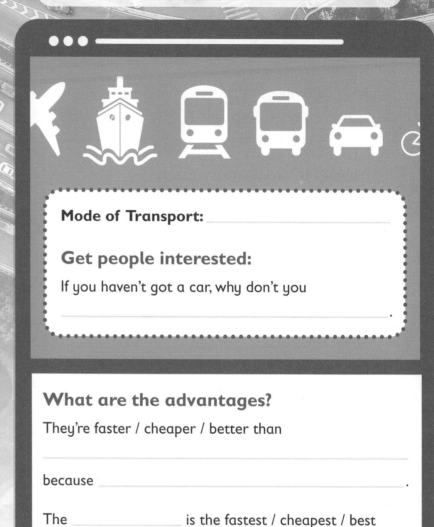

Mode of Transport: _____

Get people interested:

If you haven't got a car, why don't you

_____ .

What are the advantages?

They're faster / cheaper / better than

_____

because _____ .

The _____ is the fastest / cheapest / best mode of transport in the world!

You can _____ .

3 **Use your notes to create an advert for the transport.**

4 **Did you ...**
- ☐ plan your advert?
- ☐ use comparatives and superlatives?
- ☐ read your advert again?
- ☐ check grammar, spelling and punctuation?

Writing tip

We use comparatives to talk about two things.

  Trains are **faster than** buses in my city.

We use superlatives to talk about one thing from a group of the same things.

  Buses are **the cheapest** way to travel in my city.

You can use comparatives and superlatives in your advert to say why your transport is the best.

Geography: city life | 🛡 critical thinking

Flyers Listening Part 2

1 🎧 13 **Listen and write. There is one example.**

George's holiday to London

Transport:	by _____train_____
1 Hotel name:	The _____
2 Where the hotel is:	next to the British _____
3 Hotel phone number:	_____
4 Where George visited:	The _____ Theatre
5 Time of the play:	Sunday at _____

Disaster!

We use the past continuous to describe what was happening in the past.

Affirmative	Negative (n't = not)	Question
I **was listening** to music.	You **weren't playing** tennis.	**Was** she **reading**?
They **were walking** to school.	He **wasn't running** in the park.	**Were** they **sailing**?

 Match the pictures with the text.

Emma's talking to her teacher. She's saying why she was late for school.

☐ Then I saw the bus. It was coming down the street so I started to run.

☐ The books were on the road in the water when the bus ran over them.

☐ I didn't have a coat or umbrella so I decided to get the bus.

☐ Now I can't find my homework. It must be on the road. Sorry! And I'm sorry I'm late!

☐ 1 I had a disaster this morning. I was walking to school when it started to rain.

☐ When I was running for the bus I dropped my schoolbag and my books fell out onto the road.

 Write the verbs in the table. Look at the spelling.

carry   cook   cut   enjoy   get   live   lose   ~~move~~   shout   stop   swim   wake up

taking (◌ + -ing)	sailing (+ -ing)	running (x2 + -ing)
moving		

Read and choose the right words.

1 They were sailing across the lake (when) / because it started to rain.
2 He was **climb** / **climbing** in the mountains when it started to snow.
3 My dad was having a shower when the phone **ring** / **rang**.
4 The boy **was** / **were** flying his kite when he hurt his elbow.
5 They were losing **if** / **when** he scored the goal.

⏵ Do the online activities on Practice Extra as you complete this unit

Write questions and answers about Akash's day.

1 What was Akash doing at twenty past three?   He was catching the bus.

2 _____   _____

3 _____   _____

4 _____   _____

5 _____   _____

6 _____   _____

Read and complete the table.

Last week somebody broke a chair in the classroom during playtime. The children don't want to tell the teacher who broke the chair, so the teacher is trying to find out.

Oliver was wearing a red sweater and a long scarf. Freya was wearing a short skirt and green shoes. Katy was wearing jeans and a T-shirt. Kito was wearing grey trousers and a blue shirt.

The girl wearing jeans was jumping around the classroom. The boy wearing a blue shirt was playing football outside. One girl was reading a book in the playground. Oliver was talking to his friends in the playground. The child who broke the chair wasn't wearing green shoes or grey trousers.

Name	Oliver			
Clothes				
Where?				
What doing?				

Who broke the chair? _____

1 Choose dates from the box to label the pictures.

> 6 May 1937   14 April 1912   28 December 1908
> 26 August 1883   10–16 October 1780   ~~1 November 1755~~

1 November 1755 _____   _____

2 Read and write the dates.

1 The day before the twenty-fifth.
   The twenty-fourth.

2 The day after the twenty-first.
   _____

3 The day after the twenty-fourth.
   _____

4 This day is three days after the twenty-sixth.
   _____

5 This is the day after the twenty-third.
   _____

6 This day is three days before the thirtieth.
   _____

3 Complete the sentences.

1 The first month is
   January   .

2 The third month is
   _____ .

3 The fifth month is
   _____ .

4 The seventh month is
   _____ .

5 The eleventh month is
   _____ .

6 The twelfth month is
   _____ .

4 Look and complete the months. Put them in order.

A _____

J __ e

S _____

O _____

M _____

D _____

M ____

1 J a n u a r y

J _____

A _____

N _____

F _____

Vocabulary: disasters and months

Answer the questions.

1   What date was it yesterday? It was _____
2   What date is it going to be next Saturday? _____
3   When's your birthday? _____
4   When's your friend's birthday? _____
5   When's your teacher's birthday? _____
6   What date does school finish this term? _____

 Match the words with the pictures.

1 storm	2 tsunami	3 ice	4 hurricane
5 volcano	6 fog	7 fire	8 lightning

 Now match the words and pictures with the definitions.

a   Heavy rain and strong winds. [1]

b   Very cold water which is solid, not liquid. [ ]

c   A mountain with a big hole at the top through which liquid rock and hot gas can come out. [ ]

d   Electricity in the air which passes from one cloud to another or to the ground. [ ]

e   Burning material and gases which can burn other things. [ ]

f   A cloud which is near the ground or the sea. [ ]

g   An enormous and fast wave. [ ]

h   This is the worst kind of storm, with very strong winds and heavy rain. [ ]

Sounds and life skills
Thinking creatively
Pronunciation focus

1 🎧 14 **Follow the /eɪ/ sounds. Listen and check.**

wave	train	Sarah	glass	lazy	straight	lake
taxi	station	diary	parrot	safe	carrot	motorway
map	April	break	bank	waiter	camel	dangerous
jam	August	rainbow	land	surname	maths	brave
airport	farm	email	today	Katy	path	thank

2 🎧 15 **Write the words next to their vowel sounds. Listen and check.**

> ~~cheap~~ do dry feet food grey glue ~~hole~~ ~~ice~~ kind knee light
> ~~May~~ please rain sofa science ~~shoes~~ skate snow toes throw

A /eɪ/ _____ May _____

E /iː/ _____ cheap _____

I /aɪ/ _____ ice _____

O /əʊ/ _____ hole _____

U /uː/ _____ shoes _____

3 🎧 16 **Use words from Activity 2 to make the rhymes. Listen and check.**

1 Why didn't you fly your kite today?
Because it was cloudy, and the sky
was ____ grey ____ .

2 It's sunny and windy. Can I fly my kite?
Yes, get the blue one! It's nice and
_____ .

3 Why didn't you go out and play in the snow?
Because yesterday I fell and hurt my
_____ .

4 We can't find the glue! We can't find the glue!
We broke Mum's cup! What shall we
_____ ?

4 **Read, look and answer. Your words don't have to rhyme.**

1 Why didn't you swim in the sea?

_____

2 Why didn't you bake your friend a cake?

_____

3 Why didn't you go to the funfair?

_____

Read and answer.

Diggory Bones

1 What does 'Canis Major' mean? It means 'the big dog'.
2 What's the brightest star called? _____
3 What was the date in the story? _____
4 When did Diggory remember the disaster? _____
5 What destroyed Ancient Alexandria? _____
6 What came after the volcanic eruption? _____

 Complete the sentences from the story. Match them with the pictures.

~~date~~ dangerous hot light secret storm

1 What's the ____date____ today, Emily?
2 Night's falling and a _____'s coming.
3 Is it too _____ for you, Bones?
4 Today, it's going to show us the 'opening' of the _____ cave!
5 It's really _____ down here.
6 Run to the _____, Emily!

Do you remember?

1 It's very difficult to see when the weather is ____foggy____ .
2 We sometimes see _____ in the sky when there's a storm.
3 Today's date in numbers is _____ .
4 Tomorrow's date in words is _____ .
5 Two words with the 'o' sound are _____ and _____ .
6 Two words with the 'u' sound are _____ and _____ .

Can do

I can talk about the weather and disasters.

I can talk about things that were happening in the past.

I can write a story.

Where can we find volcanoes?

1 **Read and match.**

1 During the summer holiday, I visited Santa Maria del Oro,

2 It's on a dormant volcano,

3 There are pools of thermal water around the lake,

4 You can eat out in one of the restaurants,

a which often serve fresh fish from the lake.

b which is a town in the state of Nayarit in Mexico.

c which people swim in because it's healthy.

d which is famous for its beautiful lake in the crater.

2 **Plan to write an email. Complete the information about a famous place you visited.**

Who are you writing to?	Hi _____,
Where did you go?	During the summer holiday, I visited _____.
What's it famous for?	_____ is a _____ in _____, which is famous for its _____.
What can you see / do there?	In _____ you can see _____, which _____. There are also _____.
Would you like to go back? Why?	I hope I can go back to / you can visit _____ one day because it's _____.
Ending	See you soon, _____

3 **Use your notes to write an email to a partner about the place.**

4 **Did you …**

☐ plan your email?
☐ use **which** to give extra information?
☐ start and end your email correctly?
☐ read your email again?
☐ check grammar, spelling and punctuation?

1 **Emma's talking to her friend David about what he did last night.**
What does David say to Emma?

Read the conversation and choose the best answer.
Write a letter (A–E) for each answer.
There is one example.

Example

 Emma: Did you watch TV last night?

 David: _____ D _____

Questions

1   **Emma:** What did you watch?

 David: _____

2   **Emma:** What was it about?

 David: _____

3   **Emma:** Really, was there anything on earthquakes?

David: _____

4   **Emma:** What time did it finish?

 David: _____

A Yes, there was. It was really amazing.
B I watched a documentary.
C It wasn't late. It finished at seven o'clock.
D Yes, I did. **(Example)**
E It was all about natural disasters.

1 **Read the story. Choose words from the box to complete the sentences.**

> corner   left   ~~March~~   quarter   restaurant   right
> straight   theatre   walking   wasn't   were

FRIENDLY

Last Saturday, 30 (1)_____March_____, was Jim's birthday. He decided to go to the city centre with Peter to have lunch in an expensive (2)_____ and to go to the cinema to see a film. They went to the station at (3)_____ past nine on Saturday morning and caught the train from platform 1. They didn't know the city very well and they didn't have a map so they decided to explore.

When they were walking along a long road, they turned (4)_____ , not right, and got lost. When they were trying to find the right street, they saw hotels, post offices, gyms and museums, but no restaurants. At ten past two, they found a small café. They were really hungry, so they stopped there and had a burger and chips for lunch. When they got to the cinema, they found it (5)_____ showing the action film they wanted to see – it was showing a cartoon about funny animals for very young children.

They were (6)_____ back to the station when it started to rain heavily and they didn't have any coats. Jim thought that his birthday was the biggest disaster ever, but then Peter started to laugh loudly and they agreed it was the funniest birthday ever.

2 **Choose a title for this episode of Friendly.**

a The best day   b The wrong map   c What a disaster!

3 **Find the odd one out and write why.**

1 across   past   (museum)   behind
   Museum because it's a building.

2 hotel   taxi   restaurant   theatre
   _____

3 stadium   left   between   right
   _____

4 lightning   rain   snow   tsunami
   _____

5 sailed   ran   flew   help
   _____

6 February   Thursday   April   October
   _____

4 **Complete the sentences. Count and write the letters.**

1 This is smaller than a road. It's a ___street___ . [6]

2 The lightning _____ their boat. [ ]

3 The opposite of inside is _____ . [ ]

4 The tenth month is _____ . [ ]

5 There was a forest _____ last summer. It burned everything. [ ]

6 The place where we go to catch a plane is an _____ . [ ]

7 Cloud on the ground is called _____ . [ ]

8 The month that comes before September is _____ . [ ]

9 There's a _____ when there's heavy rain and a strong wind. [ ]

10 We go to a _____ to see old books and paintings. [ ]

11 We use a _____ to help us find our way. [ ]

12 The point where two streets meet is a _____ . [ ]

13 We need a _____ to walk over a river. [ ]

14 The first month is _____ . [ ]

5 **Now complete the crossword. Write the message.**

m 5

3

7

6

c

¹s t r e e t

A

4

2

1	2	3	4	4	2	1		5	6	4	5	7
S						S							!

6 **Quiz time!**

1 What's the name of the busiest airport in the UK? _The busiest airport is_ _____

2 When was the cable car system in Medellín built? _____

3 What was Stella's dad listening to on the boat? _____

4 What do we call dangerous storms with strong winds? _____

5 Where are more than 75% of the Earth's volcanoes? _____

7 **Write questions for your quiz in your notebook.**

5 Material things

We use *made of* to describe materials.

Affirmative	Negative (n't = not)	Question
It's **made of** chocolate.	It isn't **made of** paper.	Is it **made of** sugar?
They're **made of** stone.	They aren't **made of** wood.	Are they **made of** leaves?

1 Match the words with the pictures.

~~bone~~ bricks grass leaves paper stone

1

bone

2

3

4

5

6

2 Read and order the words.

1 made / This / is / jacket / fur. / of
   This jacket is made of fur.

2 isn't / skirt / That / made / chocolate. / of

3 your / of? / sweater / made / What's

4 T-shirt / your / Is / of / made / fur?

5 made / of / their / shoes / Are / wood?

6 paper. / clothes / made / are / of / His

3 Correct the sentences.

1 My hat~~s~~ is made of fur.
2 The spider has made of paper.
3 The cake aren't made of chocolate.
4 Is his jacket made off rubber?
5 Are their houses mades of stone?
6 My sweets is made of sugar.

4 What are they made of? Look and write.

1

2

They're made of chocolate.

3

4

5

6

Write the correct sentences.

Our house	made	of paper.
The boat is	is made	of rubber.
My book's	are made	of stone.
Their tyres	made of	wood.

1 _____
2 _____
3 _____
4 _____

 Read, look and label the picture.

My house is made of trees and it's got grass on the roof. Grass is really good because it's very green. The house stays hot in the winter and cold in the summer. When it snows, I can ski on it!

The door is made of wood. The windows are made of water bottles. When it rains, the water from the roof goes into the window bottles. I use it to water my plants. There are leaves over the balcony. I can sit under these when it's sunny.

1   house made of trees
2 _____

3 _____
4 _____
5 _____

 Read and complete the text.   bottles   bridges   gold   ~~materials~~   stone   thousand

The Romans were the first people to use a lot of different
(1) _____materials_____ , both for building and in their everyday life.
They were very good at making things from a lot of different metals,
including (2)_____ and silver.

They made a lot of things with glass, like (3)_____ and
glasses for drinking.

The Romans made houses from wood, (4)_____ and
concrete. They also built 50,000 kilometres of roads and were the first
people to be really good at making (5)_____ .
The first bridge with a name was the Pons Fabricius and it was made of
stone. They built it over the River Tiber in Rome in 62 BC and it's there
today, two (6)_____ years later.

1 Choose words from the box to label the pictures.

card ~~glass~~ gold metal paper plastic silver wood wool

1 _glass_   2 _____   3 _____   4 _____   5 _____   6 _____

2 Find and write eight materials.

p	a	p	e	r	y	w	u	a	p
l	s	c	o	s	i	l	v	e	r
a	k	t	a	m	a	t	l	c	b
s	a	o	d	r	f	e	q	o	w
t	w	t	n	f	d	a	i	l	o
i	g	o	l	d	u	a	h	t	o
c	n	m	o	v	m	e	t	a	l
d	c	p	o	d	t	r	t	g	k

1 g _o_ _l_ _d_   5 c _____
2 s _____   6 p _____
3 p _____   7 m _____
4 w _____ d   8 w _____ l

3 Write the words.

1 A man-made material. We make it from oil.
   plastic

2 An expensive white metal. _____

3 Animal hair. _____

4 Windows are made of this. It can break easily.
   _____

5 We get this material from sheep.
   _____

6 An expensive yellow metal. _____

7 The material we write on in our notebooks.
   _____

8 This material is made from wood. It's thicker
   than paper. _____

4 Look at the letters on the clock and write the words.

1 It's twenty-five past twelve.   _gold_

2 It's ten to three.   _____

3 It's twenty to two.   _____

4 It's half past four.   _____

5 It's quarter to eleven.   _____

6 It's twenty to two.   _____

ld
ver   at
wo   rd
sil   od
ca   tal
co   go
me

1 Read. Change one letter to write a new word.

face	Part of our body, on the front of our head.
race	A competition to see who's the fastest.
	Something we eat.
	Good, lovely.
	A number between eight and ten.
	My things, something I've got.
	A straight mark on a page or drawing.
	The opposite of **don't like**.
	Where do you … ?
	The opposite of **hate**.
	We do this with our body when we dance.
	Gold is … expensive than silver.
	The past of **wear**.
	The opposite of **play**.
	Part of a sentence.
	We get this material from trees.
	We get this material from sheep.
pool	Somewhere we can go to swim.

 2 Now write the clues for this puzzle.

well	The opposite of 'badly'.
wall	
ball	
tall	
talk	
walk	

 3 Find eight mistakes in the text.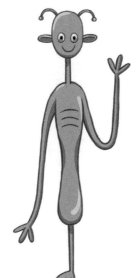

Glook's from a different world. He's doing a project about Earth and there are a lot of mistakes. Can you help him to correct his homework?

People on Earth use things which are made of different materials. Plastic, wood and (dictionaries) are all different materials. Bottles are made of glass or paper. Tables and chairs can be made of fog, cloud or metal. People on Earth like reading books, comics and volcanoes. These are made of card and wool. Earth people get wool from parrots. I'm going to visit Earth next November. I want to get a lovely big bracelet made of water. I can wear it when I go to parties.

 4 Now write the text correctly.

People on Earth use things which are made of different materials. Plastic, wood and card are all different materials.

Sounds and life skills

Talking about different ideas

Pronunciation focus

1 🎧 **17** **Listen and complete.**

1 ___Look at___ this!
Wow! That's amazing!

2 _____!
I'm coming!

3 _____!
Ouch!

4 I've got _____ great _____!
What is it?

5 _____ star!
I know!

2 🎧 **18** **Look and match. Then listen and circle the connected letters.**

1 chocola(te e)ggs
2 two glass eyes
3 purple ice cream
4 lots of red apples
5 an insect made of sugar

3 🎧 **19** **Choose a phrase from Activity 1. Listen and check.**

4 **Complete the comic strip. Add speech bubbles using phrases from Activity 1.**

1

Look at this!

2

3

Nice!

4

Two friends go to a funfair.
Look! There's a funfair!
Let's go and see!

They visit a joke tent with lots of fun things to look at.

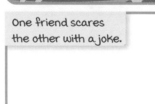
One friend scares the other with a joke.

And then ...

1 Read and answer.

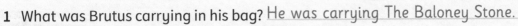

1 What was Brutus carrying in his bag? <u>He was carrying The Baloney Stone.</u>
2 What's the inside of Brutus's bag made of? _____
3 What did Brutus push? _____
4 Why's it dangerous to joke about Sirius? _____
5 What are the bowls made of? _____
6 What does Brutus want? _____

2 Read and order the text.

in his bag, but The Baloney Stone's safe ☐

because the inside's made of plastic. Diggory ☐

Brutus is carrying the computer 1

the instructions. Brutus pushes the picture ☐

Cleopatra's treasure from her underwater palace. ☐

of the snake and a secret door opens. They ☐

find a lot of treasure behind the wall. It's ☐

understands the writing on the wall and reads ☐

1 Trees are made of ____wood____ .
2 Scarves are made of _____ .
3 Gold and silver are precious _____ .
4 My friend is afraid _____ spiders.
5 Complete the phrase: 'You're a _____.'
6 Complete the phrase: 'Wait a _____.'

Can do

I can talk about materials.

I can talk about what things are made of.

I can write a description of my classroom.

What can you make with recycled materials?

1 **Read and circle the adverbs.**

The Singing Ringing Tree

This sculpture is called the Singing Tree. I saw it in England when I was on holiday. It's (really) interesting because it's a sculpture but it sings too!

It's made of metal pipes in the shape of a tree. It's an amazing sculpture because the sun shines brightly on the pipes. When the wind blows gently through the pipes, we can hear beautiful music.

I love the idea because the sculpture shows nature, and the wind makes it alive. When I hear the sculpture sing, I'm completely relaxed. It's a clever idea to mix man-made materials with nature.

2 **Plan to write a review. Complete the information about an interesting sculpture.**

Name of sculpture

Where is it?

What materials does it use?

What's interesting or different about it?

What idea does the sculpture show?

It's called _____.

I saw the sculpture _____.

The sculpture is made of _____.

There is / are _____.

It's interesting / different because _____.

_____ is my favourite because

_____.

I love the way the artist _____.

The sculpture shows _____.

3 **Use your notes to write a review of the sculpture.**

4 **Did you ...**

- [ ] plan your review?
- [ ] use adverbs?
- [ ] read your review again?
- [ ] check grammar, spelling and punctuation?

Writing tip

We use adverbs to describe how we do something.

I love the way the artist **skilfully** joined all the objects together.

We can also use them to make our ideas and feelings stronger.

When I hear the sculpture sing, I'm **completely** relaxed.

Art: sculptures | creative thinking

Flyers Listening Part 3

1 🎧 20 **Whose things are these?**

Listen and write a letter in each box. There is one example.

 Sarah [E]    Robert [ ]    Emma [ ]    Richard [ ]    Katy [ ]    Michael [ ]

A

B

C

D

E

F

6 Senses

What ... like?

We use verb + *like* to describe things.

Affirmative	Negative (n't = not)	Question
It **looks like** a ball.	It **doesn't sound like** a car.	**What** does it **feel like**?
It **smells like** a lemon.	It **doesn't taste like** chocolate.	**What** does it **look like**?

 Read and order the words.

1 blue cheese / smells / That / old / horrible.
   That old blue cheese smells horrible.

2 it's / rain. / going to / It / looks / like

_____

3 smartphone. / That / like / your / sounds

_____

4 like? / does / this / toy mouse / What / feel

_____

5 Her / cake / coffee. / tastes / like

_____

6 look / like? / What / my picture / does

_____

 Correct the sentences.

1 Your smartphone sound^s like a frog.
2 My sweater doesn't feels like fur.
3 That pen look likes a banana.

4 This biscuit don't taste like chocolate.
5 What does that cheese smells like?
6 I doesn't look like my dad.

 Read and complete the email.

exciting   feel   felt   hear   quickly   ~~Saturday~~   shouting

---

Hi Frank,

How was your weekend? I had a really good one because on ⁽¹⁾ _Saturday_ we went to a new theme park. It's really
⁽²⁾ _____ and has got lots of things to do. Can you see the picture of the rollercoaster? It's amazing!
That's me ⁽³⁾ _____ loudly. I thought it looked dangerous, but I didn't
⁽⁴⁾ _____ afraid. It sounded very loud, though – I couldn't ⁽⁵⁾ _____
anything.

I also went on a big wheel. You sit in a chair and it goes round and round very
⁽⁶⁾ _____ . At first I felt excited, but then I felt sick. When I got off I didn't
feel very well. I ⁽⁷⁾ _____ ill, but I liked it.

Let's speak soon.

Richard

Language: describing sensations with *feel, taste, smell, look, sound*

Do the online activities on Practice Extra
as you complete this unit

How do they look? Write the answers.

1 She looks pleased.   4 _____

2 _____   5 _____

3 _____   6 _____

 **Read. What are they?**

1 It looks like an apple, but it isn't round. It's green or yellow. What is it?   _a pear_

2 It looks like a bean, but it isn't. It's green, small and round. What is it? _____

3 It's a fruit and it tastes like a lime, but it isn't green. It's yellow. What is it? _____

4 It's a hot drink. Some people have it with sugar and milk. It sometimes looks like coffee, but it doesn't taste like coffee. What is it? _____

5 They sometimes taste like burgers. They're long and thin. What are they? _____

6 This sounds like a lion, but it isn't. It's got orange fur and black stripes. What is it? _____

 Senses quiz. Read and answer.

www.lottaquizzes

1 Which part of the body do we use to taste?   Our tongue. _____
2 Which part of the body do we use to smell?   _____
3 Which parts of the body do we use to see?   _____
4 Which parts of the body do we use to hear?   _____
5 Which parts of the body can we use to touch things? _____
6 What are your favourite sounds?   _____
7 What smells make you hungry?   _____
8 Which of your senses do you think is the strongest? _____

Language: describing sensations with *feel, taste, smell, look, sound*   55

Look and complete the words.

p _e_ p _p_ _e_ r

s _ _ t

k n _ _ _ _ _

f _ _ _ k

s p _ _ _ _

p _ _ t _

 Look and find the words.

There are 20 words.

Nine are food words. What are they? _chips,_ _____

Seven are verbs (two have two words). What are they? _____

Two are things we eat with. What are they? _____

One is a preposition. What is it? _____

One is somewhere we go to eat. What is it? _____

 Read and write the words in the puzzle.

1 We put this on our food. It's black or white. _____ pepper _____

2 We use this with a knife when we eat. _____

3 We use this in cooking. It's white. We get it from the sea or the ground. _____

4 Famous Italian food. _____

5 We put our food on this when we eat. _____

6 Bread is made of this. _____

7 We use this to cut meat. _____

8 We use this to eat ice cream. _____

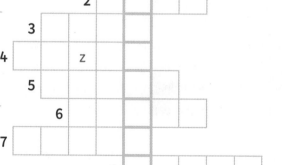

What's the mystery vegetable? _____

1 Read and complete the text.

| 900 cook cheese flour Italy largest made |
| meal metres ~~people~~ pizzas taste top |

The (1) ___people___ from Naples (Napoli) in (2) _____

were the first to make (3) _____ . Their pizzas are

(4) _____ of a bread base, with (5) _____ , tomato

and olives on top. Pizzas are people's favourite (6) _____ all

over the world, not only in Italy, because they (7) _____

delicious. Some pizzas can have extra things on (8) _____ .

They can have thicker bases and sometimes the (9) _____

can fold the pizza in half and fill it with more cheese and things. They cook pizzas in an oven.

The (10) _____ pizza ever made was in South Africa in 1990. It was enormous! It was 37.4

(11) _____ across and was made with 500 kg of (12) _____ , 800 kg of cheese and

(13) _____ kg of tomatoes. Amazing!

ITALY

NAPLES

2 Read and order the text.

	programmes. When his family came home, it looked like the kitchen was on
	were out. He decided to cook sausages and potatoes. He turned on the
1	Tom's 14. Last Saturday he decided to make lunch for his family while they
	into the hot water. He did this because sugar looks like salt and he didn't read
6	the label on the box. Then he went into the living room to watch TV while he
	to turn on the clock. Then he started to cook the potatoes, but he put sugar
	was waiting for the food to cook, and started to watch one of his favourite
9	fire. When they opened the oven, the sausages looked small and black. The
	potatoes were OK, but they tasted sweet. Tom's mum said he invented sweet potatoes!
	oven and when it felt hot, he put the sausages inside, but he forgot

Sounds and life skills
Describing senses and feelings
Pronunciation focus

 1 🎧 **21** **Listen and circle the stressed words.**

1 hot chocolate (blue cheese) sandwiches cakes **3** Sam Suzie stomach-ache swimming
2 fruit pineapple schoolbag snack box **4** guitar piano class school

 2 🎧 **22** **Listen again and complete.**

1 I don't like ___blue___ ___cheese___ in my _____!
2 _____ taking _____ in my _____!
3 _____ well. She's _____.
4 I'm _____.

 3 🎧 **23** **Listen and complete.**

My ___birthday___
It looks like colourful _____ and candles,
It tastes like birthday _____,
It smells like _____ after I blow them out,
It sounds like my _____ laughing and having _____,
If feels like a _____ from my _____.

4 **Look at the pictures and write.**

It feels like …   It looks like …   It sounds like …
It smells like …   It tastes like …

 _____
_____

 _____   _____

 _____    _____

Read and answer.

Diggory Bones

1 Where does Brutus fall? He falls into a snake bowl.
2 What's inside the snake bowl? _____
3 What does Diggory use to get Brutus out? _____
4 Who's got The Baloney Stone now? _____
5 What's the dog? _____
6 Who does Brutus push into the snake bowl? _____

Correct the sentences.

1 At first, Brutus thought that the animals felt like a mouse.
   At first, Brutus thought that the animals felt like a spider.

2 The dangerous ancient trap is called a snake plate.
   _____

3 Brutus loves spiders.
   _____

4 The snake didn't wake up.
   _____

5 Diggory used his scarf to help Brutus out of the snake bowl.
   _____

6 Brutus thought the dog was the window.
   _____

Do you remember?

1 A lemon sometimes ___looks___ like a lime.
2 Pizza doesn't smell _____ spaghetti.
3 You need a spoon and a _____ to mix salad.
4 You need an _____ to cook pizza.
5 Underline the stressed words: 'Put your hand into this box.'
6 Underline the stressed words: 'What does it feel like?'

Can do

I can talk about the five senses.

I can plan a party.

I can write about my favourite meal.

Remember to complete the online activities for this unit on **Practice Extra**

Review: unit 6

59

How do we make noises?

1 **Read and circle the sound words.**

Sounds I hate to hear

I hate to hear a loud bell (clanging) because it gives me a headache.

I hate to hear an angry lion roaring because it makes me feel scared.

I hate to hear car horns honking outside my house because it wakes me up in the morning.

But I love to hear the first school bell ringing because it means I'll see my friends!

BEEP!!!
BEEP!!!

2 **Plan to write a poem. Complete the information about sounds you love and hate.**

Sounds I love to hear)))

I love to hear _____ because it means _____ .

I love to hear _____ because it means _____ .

I love to hear _____ because it makes me feel _____ .

I love to hear _____ because it makes me feel _____ .

But I hate to hear _____ because _____ .

3   **Use your notes to write a poem.**

4 **Did you ...**

☐ plan your poem?

☐ use sound words?

☐ read your poem again?

☐ check grammar, spelling and punctuation?

Writing tip

Sound words sound like their meanings. You can use them in your poem to help the reader hear the sounds you are writing about.

I hate to hear lions **roaring** because it makes me feel scared.

I love to hear plates **clattering** in the kitchen because it means dinner is nearly ready.

Science: sound waves | critical thinking

Flyers Reading and Writing Part 5

1 **Look at the picture and read the story. Write some words to complete the sentences about the story. You can use 1, 2, 3 or 4 words.**

Helen is twelve and she's got a brother called William, who's six. Last Saturday Helen's dad took them to an art museum in the city centre. They were very pleased. There was a show of modern art by a famous artist and the museum was full of people. Helen was standing in front of a painting, looking at it when William said, 'This looks like a really big pizza with small tomatoes and olives on it.'

Helen said, 'You don't understand modern art, William. This is a great painting that shows us that life is beautiful, but difficult.' Helen's dad laughed and said, 'I think William understands modern art better than you, Helen. Look!' Helen's dad pointed and Helen saw the title of the painting. It was called 'Pizza with tomatoes and olives'.

Example

Helen's brother _____is six_____ years old.

Questions

1 Helen's got _____ called William.

2 Last Saturday Helen and William _____ art museum with their father.

3 The show was by a famous artist and there were a lot of _____ at the museum.

4 One painting _____ like a really big pizza.

5 Helen's dad read the title of the _____ .

1 **Read the story. Choose words from the box to complete the sentences.**

~~competition~~ felt film flour like made
pizza plastic sounded touch were

FRIENDLY

Last November Frankie won an important art (1) __competition__ for her painting Modern Girl, which she said looked
(2) _____ Jenny. The prize was a meal for two in Luigi's, the town's best Italian restaurant.

Frankie invited Jenny to have lunch with her. Jenny felt very pleased. She bought a new dress which was (3) _____ of bright yellow wool. She wore it with a big brown (4) _____ belt and a dark brown jacket. She looked like a 'Modern Girl' and she (5) _____

like a film star. The two friends felt hungry when they arrived at the restaurant. The waiter put their (6) _____ on the table and they agreed it smelled like the best in the world. When they were eating it, they said it tasted like nothing on Earth – it was delicious. After the pizza, Luigi came out of the kitchen and carefully put the second course on the table. It was his most famous sweet, 'Banana and Chocolate Surprise'. Frankie and Jenny felt very surprised. It looked just like Jenny's clothes!

2 **Choose a title for this episode of Friendly.**

   a The cook's famous clothes   **b** A sweet dress   **c** Jenny looks like a pear

3 **Find the odd one out and write why.**

   1 silver metal gold (plastic)
     Plastic because it isn't a metal.

   2 salt olives wool pepper

   3 eyes feel taste smell

   4 spoon bracelet knife fork

   5 wool hair stone fur

   6 wood paper card glass

4 Complete the sentences. Count and write the letters.

1 Her smartphone _____sounds_____ like a baby laughing. [6]

2 We've got five senses. They are sight, hearing, touch, smell and _____. [ ]

3 We use a _____ to cut meat. [ ]

4 _____ is a material we get from sheep. [ ]

5 The opposite of strong is _____. [ ]

6 What does that cloud look _____? [ ]

7 We hear with our _____. [ ]

8 We use a _____ to eat soup. [ ]

9 _____ is an expensive white metal. [ ]

10 Knives and forks can be made of metal or _____. [ ]

11 _____ is a material we get from trees. [ ]

12 What's your bracelet _____ of? Metal. [ ]

13 We feel _____ if we don't drink. [ ]

14 We serve food on a _____. [ ]

5 Now complete the crossword. Write the message.

s
o
u
n
d
s

2   10

³u

9

1   e

6

7

p

⁵d

8

⁴

1	2	3	4	5	1
	u				

6	7	8	9		10	3	4
						u		**!**

6 Quiz time!

1 What's Lenny's spider made of?
Lenny's spider is made of fur.

2 What's Arsenault's house made of?
_____

3 Where can you see the giant tap scuplture?
_____

4 What smells like Lenny's socks?
_____

5 What does Luigi's Italian restaurant make?
_____

6 What's the loudest sound on Earth?
_____

7 Write questions for your quiz in your notebook.

7 Natural world

We use *should* to give and ask for help or advice.

Affirmative	Negative (n't = not)	Question
I **should look after** the countryside.	You **shouldn't throw** rubbish on the ground.	**Should** he **help** his mum in the garden?
She **should tidy up** her room.	We **shouldn't forget** that we only have one world.	**Should** they **drive** a big car?

1 Read and match.

1 What should you wear if you go for a long walk?
2 What should you wear outdoors on a sunny day?
3 What should you wear when it's very cold?
4 Who should you ask if you get lost in a big city?
5 What should you do when you cross the road?
6 Why should you use sun cream?

☐ You should wear a coat and scarf.
☐ You should stop and look both ways.
☐ 1 You should wear strong shoes.
☐ To protect your skin from the sun.
☐ You should ask a police officer.
☐ You should wear a hat.

2 Think and write 'should' or 'shouldn't'.

1 It's a sunny day and Yu Xi's at the beach. She _____should_____ wear a hat.
2 Michael's got a headache. He _____ watch TV.
3 Nadia's got a terrible toothache. She _____ go to the dentist.
4 Fahad wants to cross the road. He _____ stop and look both ways first.
5 Anika _____ eat chocolate because she's got a stomach-ache.
6 Hiroto's got an important exam tomorrow, so he _____ study this afternoon.

3 Correct the sentences.

1 We've should look after the countryside. <u>We should look after the countryside.</u>
2 We should to walk on the paths. _____
3 We should drop our rubbish. _____
4 We always should use bins. _____
5 We shouldn't of play with animals in fields. _____
6 We's shouldn't drink water from rivers. _____

☐ Do the online activities on **Practice Extra** as you complete this unit

1 Match the problems with the correct advice.

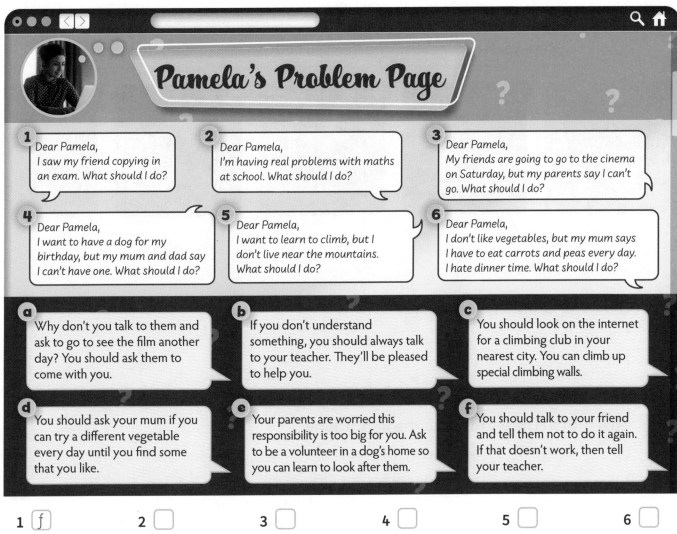

Pamela's Problem Page

1 Dear Pamela,
I saw my friend copying in an exam. What should I do?

2 Dear Pamela,
I'm having real problems with maths at school. What should I do?

3 Dear Pamela,
My friends are going to go to the cinema on Saturday, but my parents say I can't go. What should I do?

4 Dear Pamela,
I want to have a dog for my birthday, but my mum and dad say I can't have one. What should I do?

5 Dear Pamela,
I want to learn to climb, but I don't live near the mountains. What should I do?

6 Dear Pamela,
I don't like vegetables, but my mum says I have to eat carrots and peas every day. I hate dinner time. What should I do?

a Why don't you talk to them and ask to go to see the film another day? You should ask them to come with you.

b If you don't understand something, you should always talk to your teacher. They'll be pleased to help you.

c You should look on the internet for a climbing club in your nearest city. You can climb up special climbing walls.

d You should ask your mum if you can try a different vegetable every day until you find some that you like.

e Your parents are worried this responsibility is too big for you. Ask to be a volunteer in a dog's home so you can learn to look after them.

f You should talk to your friend and tell them not to do it again. If that doesn't work, then tell your teacher.

1 [f]   2 [ ]   3 [ ]   4 [ ]   5 [ ]   6 [ ]

2 Think and write advice for someone …

1 … who's going to the beach on a hot day.
2 … who's got a headache.
3 … who wants to learn English.
4 … who wants to try a new hobby.
5 … who wants to learn more about the past.
6 … who is always fighting with their brother.

1 You should take a hat and sun cream. You shouldn't lie in the sun all day.

3 Answer the questions.

1 Do your friends talk to you when they have a problem? _____

2 Do you help your friends? _____

3 Do you think you should always keep secrets? _____

4 Who do you talk to when you have a problem? _____

5 What are the biggest problems for you and your friends? _____

6 When should you tell your teacher about a problem? _____

1 Choose words from the box to label the pictures.

> Lehmann's poison frog ~~Mountain zebra~~
> Nine-spotted ladybird   Purple spotted butterfly   Siberian tiger

Mountain
zebra

_____ _____ _____ _____

2 Look and complete the words.

1 w i n g s
2 b _ tt _ _ f _ _
3 in _ _ c _

4 s p _ _
5 st _ _ p _
6 f _ _

7 t _ _ l
8 b _ _ y
9 b _ _ tl _

3 Now match the words with the definitions.

1 _____beetle_____   This insect has got two hard wings and two soft wings.
2 _____   The hair an animal has on its body.
3 _____   The parts of an insect or animal which it uses to fly.
4 _____   Lions, tigers, elephants and mice all have one of these. It comes out of the back part of their bodies.
5 _____   The part of an animal or insect which has the arms and legs on it.
6 _____ . An insect with two beautiful wings, six legs and two antennae.
7 _____   A small animal with a body, six legs and two eyes.
8 _____   A small coloured circle on a different colour.
9 _____   An area between two lines which is a different colour.

4 Write the words in the table.

> across   appear   ~~become~~   explore   extinct   extinction   ~~funny~~
> into   over   recycle   ~~spot~~   spotted   stripe   ~~through~~   striped   wing

Adjectives	Verbs	Prepositions	Nouns
funny	become	through	spot

1 **Match the pictures of endangered animals with the words.**

 a
 b
 c
 d

 e
 f
 g
 h

1	Leatherback turtle	a	
2	Orang-utan		
3	White rhino		
4	Iberian lynx		

5	Whale		
6	Giant panda		
7	Bearded vulture		
8	Bat		

2 **Now find out one fact about each of the endangered animals in Activity 1.**

Leatherback turtles live in the Pacific Ocean.

 3 **Now make a quiz for your friends.**

Endangered animals quiz

1 Where do leatherback turtles live?

4 **Read and order the story.**

☐ 'What's your question?' the teacher asked.

☐ The old man said, 'I don't know either. Here are your two pounds!'

☐ 1 One day a very clever teacher went to a small village in the country.

☐ The teacher was happy with the old man's idea because he was very clever.

☐ The teacher thought for a long time, but he didn't know the answer.

☐ 'What animal has got three heads, two wings and one leg?' the old man asked.

☐ He was talking to the people there when an old man spoke to him: 'I have a question for you. If you can't answer my question, you give me ten pounds. Then you ask me a question. If I can't answer it, I give you two pounds.'

☐ After 30 minutes thinking, he gave the old man his ten pounds and said, 'I'm sorry. I don't know the answer. What is it?'

Sounds and life skills
Taking care of your community
Pronunciation focus

 🎧 24 Listen and circle the stressed words.

1 We should (clean up) the beach.
2 People should pick up their rubbish.
3 People should put plastic rubbish in the yellow bins.
4 We should ask the council for bags.
5 People shouldn't leave rubbish on the beach.
6 Where should people throw the rubbish?

 Circle to complete the rules.

We don't say every word in a sentence with the same force. Strong words are important words, so we say them with more force.

Verbs, adjectives and nouns **are / are not** strong words.

Prepositions (*in, on, at*) **are / are not** strong words.

Negative words (*shouldn't, don't, didn't*) **are / are not** strong words.

 🎧 25 Listen and complete.

Lola: Look at this beach! There's so much rubbish!

Li Wei: We ___should___ do something!

Fahad: _____ _____ clean it up?

Lola: Good idea! We _____ ask more friends to help.

Fahad: _____ message them. We could meet next Saturday morning.

Nadia: My mum works at the council. I _____ ask for some rubbish bags and gloves.

Li Wei: Great! _____ _____ we also take photos and send them to the local newspaper?

Lola: Yes! Then people will be more responsible!

 Complete Lola's message.

~~beach~~ clean clean-up
Great newspaper photos

Hi helpers!

Just want to say a BIG thank you for all your help at the
(1) ____beach____ last weekend.
It looks so (2) _____
now! We took lots of
(3) _____ to send to
our local (4) _____ **The Evening Report.** Everyone should see how important it is to work together in the community!
Let's start planning our next
(5) _____ in Chestnut
Wood!
(6) _____ job, everyone!

Thanks again,

The Neighbourhood Clean-up Team!

1 Read and answer.

1 What animal does Bones say Brutus is? _He says he's a snake._
2 Why should Emily go down the ladder slowly and carefully? _____
3 Where does the ladder take them? _____
4 Describe the butterflies. _____
5 What shouldn't Brutus do? _____
6 What's inside the box? _____

2 Read and order the text.

At the foot of the ladder there was a big room full of butterflies. ☐

Thousands of butterflies flew off the walls to protect their young. ☐

There was a ladder under the door. They climbed slowly and carefully down it. ☐

Diggory knew how to get out. He opened a secret door. ☐

Diggory jumped into the snake bowl to save Emily. ☐ 1

The box was full of striped insects, so Brutus dropped it. ☐

When Diggory and Emily were looking at the butterflies, Brutus opened a box. ☐

The room was the famous butterfly room of Queen Hetepheres. ☐

Do you remember?

1 I've got a problem. What _____should_____ I do?
2 You _____ throw rubbish on the floor. Put it in a bin.
3 The Lost Ladybug Project asks people to take _____ of these endangered beetles.
4 Two endangered animals which have _____ are tigers and zebras.
5 Underline the strong words: 'People shouldn't throw rubbish in the lake.'
6 Underline the strong words: 'What should they do with their rubbish?'

Can do

I can describe insects and animals.

I can talk about things we should or shouldn't do.

I can write about how to look after our world.

Remember to complete the online activities for this unit on Practice Extra

Review: unit 7   69

How can we help endangered species?

1 Read and underline facts with *when*.

PROTECTING HEDGEHOGS

Hedgehogs are nocturnal animals, which means that they sleep during the day and come out at night. They have very short legs, but they can walk very far. <u>When they come out at night for food, they can walk more than 3 kilometres!</u>

They have around 5,000 spikes and when they're scared, their spikes rise up to protect them. Hedgehogs eat mostly insects and bugs. One reason why hedgehogs are endangered is that when humans use pesticides to kill insects, there are fewer insects for the hedgehogs to eat.

When hedgehogs come into your garden, you should give them cat or dog food because this is healthy for them. When hedgehogs drink milk, they get very sick, so you should never give them milk.

2 Plan to write a report. Complete the information about an endangered animal.

Title

Why are _____ important?

Why are they endangered?

How can we help?

Protecting _____

_____ are so important because _____.

When _____, _____.

They're endangered because _____.

When _____, _____.

This means the number of _____ in the world is going down.

We can help by _____. I think we should _____, but we shouldn't _____.

3 Use your notes to write a report about the endangered animal.

4 Did you …

☐ plan your report?
☐ give facts with **when**?

☐ read your report again?
☐ check grammar, spelling and punctuation?

Flyers Listening Part 1

1 🎧 **26** **Listen and draw lines. There is one example.**

Betty   Harry   Richard   George

Katy   Holly   Sarah

8 World of sport

We use the *present perfect* to talk and write about things we did and do.

Affirmative	Negative (n't = not)	Question
I've **played** tennis.	You **haven't played** volleyball.	**Has** he **played** basketball?
She's **been** skiing.	We **haven't been** swimming.	**Have** they **been** running?

1 Are these verbs regular or irregular? Write 'R' or 'I'.

arrive R   lose I   believe ____   make ____   stop ____   play ____

meet ____   catch ____   jump ____   win ____   finish ____   wash ____

2 Make negative sentences.

1 I've sailed from England to Ireland.
   I haven't sailed from England to Ireland.

2 She's won a prize.
   _____

3 They've played basketball.
   _____

4 He's climbed the highest mountain.
   _____

5 You've won the game.
   _____

6 We've made a kite.
   _____

3 Match the pictures with the text.

It's the first time she's played badminton! ☐

This is the first time you've worked in a restaurant, isn't it? ☐

It's the first time he's won a prize. [1]

Is this the first time they've washed the car? ☐

I've never made a cake before. ☐

We've never been ice skating before. ☐

Language: present perfect   ▶ Do the online activities on **Practice Extra** as you complete this unit

1 Answer the questions.

1 What's the third letter in **heard**? _a_
2 What's the second letter in **climbed**? ____
3 What's the fifth letter in **stopped**? ____
4 What's the first letter in **hockey**? ____
5 What's the third letter in **skated**? ____
6 What's the first letter in **badminton**? ____
7 What's the sixth letter in **started**? ____
8 What's the fourth letter in **football**? ____

What's the word? _____

2 Now make your word puzzle.

1 What's the seventh letter in basketball?
2 What's the first letter in appeared?

3 Write the correct form of the verbs in the email.

Hi Freya,

I'm writing to tell you about the things I've (1) ____done____ (do) in the last month or two. We haven't (2) _____ (talk) for two months. I'm sorry, but I've been really busy. I've (3) _____ (study) a lot because I've got exams next week, and at last I've (4) _____ (finish) the book which you gave me for my birthday. It was really interesting.

Let me tell you what's (5) _____ (happen) at the sports club. You know that I was in the tennis team, don't you? Well, I've (6) _____ (decide) to change sports. I've (7) _____ (stop) playing tennis and now I've (8) _____ (start) racing my bike. It's very difficult, but I like it. I've (9) _____ (race) twice, and I finished fifth and ninth. Not bad, really. Look at the photo. I'm in it!

Have you ever (10) _____ (win) a race?

Write soon!
Danny

4 Look at the pictures. Write the questions.

What have they done? _____

_____
_____

_____
_____

5 Now answer the questions.

1 They've arrived in London.
2 _____
3 _____
4 _____
5 _____
6 _____

Look and complete the words.

s k i i n g

s _ _ w b _ _ _ d i _ _ _

_ l _ _ g _ _ _ _

c _ _ l _ _ _ _

_ t h _ _ t _ _ _ _

_ _ _ f

 Write the seasons.

1 This is the hottest season. _____summer_____

2 In this season all the new flowers start growing. _____

3 This is the season when trees lose their leaves. _____

4 This is the coldest season. This season comes after autumn. _____

 Write the sports words in the table.

> athletics   basketball   cycling   horse-riding   ice hockey
> ice skating   sailing   skiing   sledging   ~~soccer~~   table tennis   tennis

Winter sports	Ball sports	Other sports
	soccer	

 What are the sports? Write the words in the puzzle.

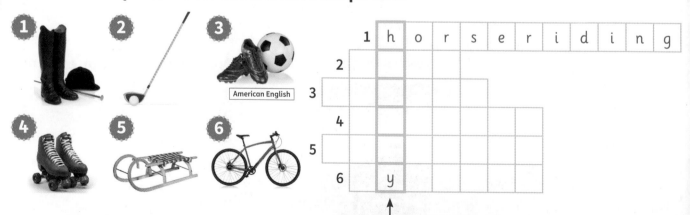

What's the mystery sport? _____

1 Write the sports.

> basketball   golf   sailing   snowboarding   ~~table tennis~~   waterskiing

1 You play inside with a small ball, two bats and a table. _table tennis_

2 This is a team game. Each team has five players. In this sport you can bounce, throw and catch the big ball.

_____

3 You do this sport on mountains when there is snow. You have to stand up to do it. _____

4 You do this sport on water. You need a boat. _____

5 You can do this on the sea or on a lake. You stand up and a boat pulls you.

_____

6 This is not a team game and you have to play outside. The players hit a very small ball around a course with 18 holes.

2 📝 Now write definitions for six more sports.

1 You usually do this sport outside. You need
a bicycle.

3 Read and complete the table.

Three friends live in houses 1, 2 and 3, next to each other in Ice Road and they have made a snowman. Where does each friend live? What has each child brought to put on the snowman?

Robert lives at number 3. He didn't bring a carrot for the snowman's nose. Sally brought a scarf for the snowman. Richard doesn't live next to Robert. One of the boys brought a hat for the snowman.

Name			Robert
House number			
Thing for the snowman			

4 📝 Choose the story. Then draw your snowman in your notebook.

Last weekend it was very cold and it snowed a lot. We went outside to play in the **park / forest / garden**. First we **played / jumped / sledged** in the snow. Then we decided to make a **big / small / tall / fat / funny / thin** snowman.

When we finished making it, we gave it a **carrot / banana / pear** for a nose and some **leaves / rocks / stones** for a mouth. Then we put an old **brown / red / purple** hat on its head and a long **spotted / striped** scarf round its neck. The scarf was **blue and green / pink and purple / red and yellow**. Finally we put two **orange / grey / black** gloves on sticks and put them into its body. The gloves were made of **leather / wool / rubber**. Our snowman looked **happy / sad / surprised / angry / amazing**. We called it

_____ .

Sounds and life skills
Working together
Pronunciation focus

 🎧 27 **Circle the word with a different -ed sound. Listen and check.**

1 opened listened (helped) rained   4 worked invited wanted waited
2 stopped arrived crossed jumped   5 finished painted washed watched
3 looked picked cooked cleaned

 🎧 28 **Listen and circle the correct -ed sound.**

1 We've climbed the highest wall in the sports centre. (/d/) /t/
2 I've finished my homework.   /d/ /t/
3 I've opened the door for my mum.   /d/ /t/
4 We've picked up the rubbish on the beach.   /d/ /t/
5 My brother's cooked pasta for dinner.   /d/ /t/
6 We've listened to music together.   /d/ /t/
7 My sister and I have washed my grandpa's car.   /d/ /t/

 Match and write for each picture.

Are you alright?   I can clean the kitchen.   Let's work together!
Would you like some help?   You're welcome!

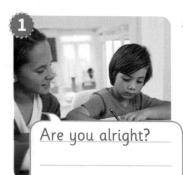

1

Are you alright?
_____

2

If you clean the
living room,
_____
_____ .

3

Thank you so much!

_____

4

_____

 🎧 29 **Read and complete with a verb from Activity 1. Listen and check.**

1 Today, I've ____helped____ my younger brother with his homework.
2 Today, we've _____ our house.
3 Today, I've _____ some clothes for my grandma.
4 Today, we've _____ on a project together.

1 Read and answer.

Diggory Bones

1 Why shouldn't Brutus open his mouth? <u>The butterflies are dangerous.</u>

2 Has Diggory ever used the new door? _____

3 Which sports did the Ancient Egyptians invent? _____

4 Where did Diggory send the email from? _____

5 What does the Ancient Story of Sirius say? _____
_____

2 Who said it? Read and match.

a They've painted sports on these walls. `3`

b It's the first time anyone's used this door. ☐

c I've waited for this moment all my life. ☐

d Now what have you done? ☐

e I haven't touched anything. ☐

f You're the 'treasure' now, Brutus! ☐

Do you remember?

1 Have you ever ___<u>been</u>___ to Egypt?

2 He's _____ the race. Now he can celebrate!

3 They haven't _____ badminton before.

4 _____ is the season which comes after spring.

5 Two words with the /t/ ending (as in 'cross<u>ed</u>') are _____ and _____ .

6 Two words with the /d/ ending (as in 'climb<u>ed</u>') are _____ and _____ .

Can do

I can talk about things I have done.

I can talk about different sports.

I can write about different sports.

How do people train for different sports?

1 **Read and complete.**

Another reason   ~~First of all~~   Lastly   Secondly

SKIING

It's never too late to try skiing, especially if you live near snowy mountains, and there are lots of reasons why it's such an amazing sport. (1) _____First of all_____ , it's an aerobic activity, which means that it helps keep you fit and healthy. (2) _____ , it's a great way to meet people and it's the perfect sport to do in a group. (3) _____ why, is that it's very good for your mental health to be in the fresh air, looking at beautiful mountains while you exercise. (4) _____ , it's great fun to be able to move quickly down the mountain.

2 **Plan to write a leaflet. Complete the information about an amazing sport.**

AMAZING SPORTS

Try _____ !

It's never too late to try _____ , and there are lots of reasons why it's such an amazing sport.

Firstly, _____ .

Secondly, _____ .

Another reason why you should try _____ is _____ .

Finally, _____ .

3 **Use your notes to write a leaflet about the sport.**

4 **Did you ...**

- ☐ plan your leaflet?
- ☐ organise your ideas?
- ☐ read your leaflet again?
- ☐ check grammar, spelling and punctuation?

Writing tip

We use **firstly, first of all, secondly, another reason is, lastly** and **finally,** to organise ideas. You can use these in your writing because they help the reader to understand your ideas more clearly.

First of all, it's an aerobic activity, which means that it helps keep you fit and healthy.

Secondly, it's a good way to meet people.

Physical education: aerobic and anaerobic exercise | collaboration

Flyers Reading and Writing Part 4

1 **Read the text. Choose the right words and write them on the lines.**

Winter sports

Example	Winter sports is the name we give to sports _____which_____
1	people do on snow. _____ sports are very popular
2	in countries where it's very cold _____ winter. One of the
3	most popular sports is skiing. There _____ three
4	kinds of _____ at the Olympic Games today. One is downhill
5	skiing, where _____ race down a hill. In another
6	kind, people _____ across the countryside. They can race
7	up to 50 kilometres. The _____ kind is ski jumping which is very
8	_____ . Skating, snowboarding and sledging are just some
9	_____ the other winter sports. At the Winter
10	Olympic Games there are _____ than ten different sports.

Example	who	when	which				
1	This	That	These	6	racing	race	races
2	in	at	on	7	three	third	thirty
3	is	are	was	8	excited	excites	exciting
4	skied	skiing	skying	9	of	at	over
5	person	people	persons	10	most	much	more

Review Units 7 and 8

1 **Read the story. Choose words from the box to complete the sentences.**

> are   coming   done   ~~ever~~   ride   skis
> sledge   snowman   taking   was   were

FRIENDLY

Have you (1) ____ever____ been skiing? This is what happened to Jim and Sally when they went last winter.

Last January the five friends went skiing with the school. On the first day, Frankie, Peter and Jenny decided that it was too dangerous for them, so they chose a sledge and found somewhere nice and quiet at the bottom of the mountain to (2) _____ on it. Jim and Sally got their skis and went quickly to the ski lift which was taking the other skiers to the top of the mountain. It was Sally's first time on a ski lift, but Jim told her it was easy and she felt really excited. They sat on the thin metal seat, held the long piece of metal which was between them and the lift started. When they (3) _____ going up the mountain, Sally fell off. She fell onto her face and stomach with her skis crossed behind her and she couldn't move. The other skiers, who were coming up on the lift behind her, couldn't stop and fell off too. Sally took her (4) _____ off to move away, but she dropped them and they fell quickly down the mountain.

Frankie, Peter and Jenny, who were sledging happily at the bottom of the mountain, suddenly saw Sally's skis coming, but they couldn't do anything and the skis hit their (5) _____. They all fell off into the snow.

On the second day, the friends decided to do something safer. They made a (6) _____!

2 **Choose a title for this episode of Friendly.**

   a Snow feels cold   **b** Snowy disaster!   **c** Summer holidays

3 **Match the questions with the answers.**

   1 What can you catch but not throw?   ☐ A watchdog.
   2 Waiter! Waiter! What's this fly doing on my ice cream?   ☐ Because 7 ate 9.
   3 Where do horses go when they feel ill?   ☐ I think it's skiing, Sir.
   4 What's worse than finding an insect in your apple?   [1] A cold.
   5 What goes 'Tick tock woof tick tock woof'?   ☐ To a horspital.
   6 Why was 10 afraid of 7?   ☐ Finding only half an insect in your apple.

4 **Complete the sentences. Count and write the letters.**

1 Snowboarding isn't easy. It's quite _difficult_ . ☐ 9

2 Have you _____ won a prize? No, never. ☐

3 When a plant or animal species doesn't exist any more, it's _____ . ☐

4 He's _____ his homework, so now he can watch TV. ☐

5 When something's got spots, it's _____ . ☐

6 What _____ they done? They've washed the car. ☐

7 When we have a picnic, we _____ pick our rubbish up. ☐

8 The T-Rex is an extinct _____ . ☐

9 Animals that fly need two _____ . ☐

10 He's the winner. He's _____ higher than the other jumpers. ☐

11 The Olympic _____ is a sports competition which is every four years. ☐

12 Zebras have got black and white _____ on their fur. ☐

13 Animal hair is called _____ . ☐

14 You play _____ on grass, hitting a small ball into holes with a long stick. ☐

5 **Now complete the crossword. Write the message.**

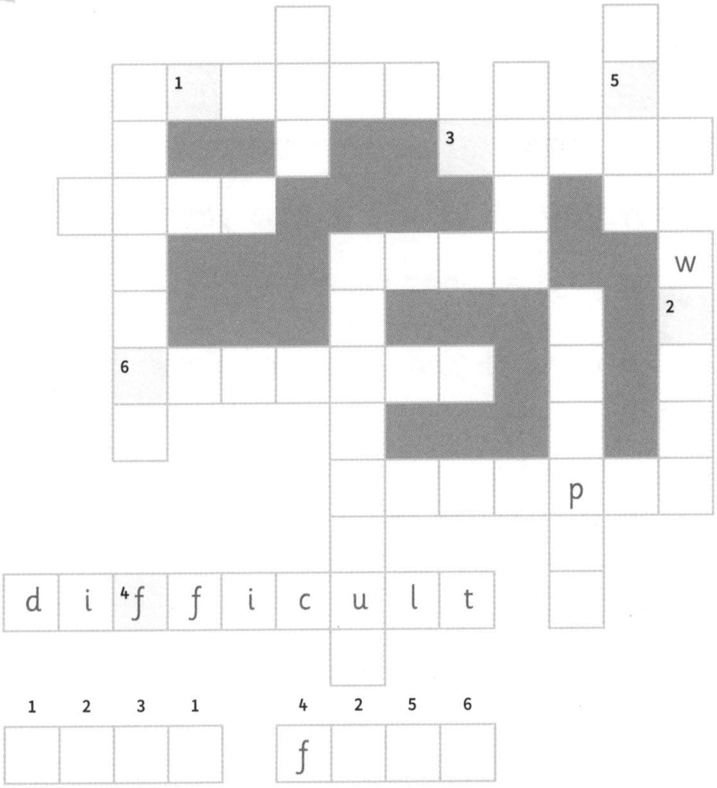

(crossword grid with clue numbers 1, 3, 5, w, 2, 6, p)

d	i	⁴f	f	i	c	u	l	t

1	2	3	1		4	2	5	6
					f			

6 **Quiz time!**

1 What should people do with their rubbish?
They should _____

2 What has two soft and two hard wings?
_____

3 Where do turtles lay their eggs?
_____

4 How many prizes has Lenny won?
_____

5 When do people go skiing?
_____

6 What sends oxygen around your body to your muscles?
_____

7 📝 **Write questions for your quiz in your notebook.**

Units 1&2 Values
Respect in the classroom

1 **Read and choose the answer.**

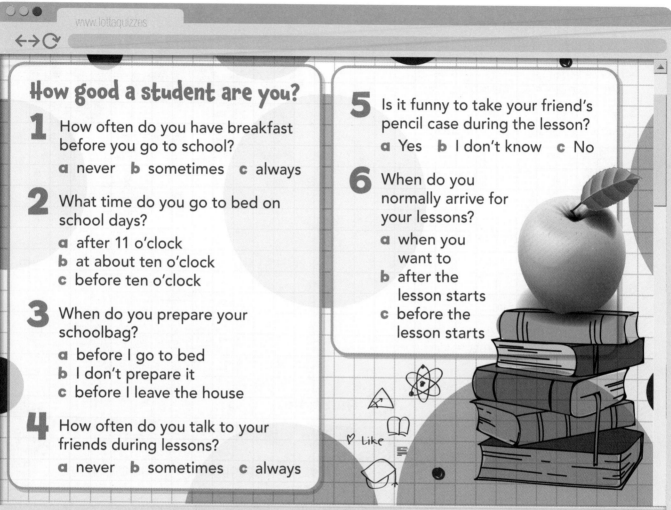

How good a student are you?

1 How often do you have breakfast before you go to school?
  a never   **b** sometimes   **c** always

2 What time do you go to bed on school days?
  a after 11 o'clock
  b at about ten o'clock
  c before ten o'clock

3 When do you prepare your schoolbag?
  a before I go to bed
  b I don't prepare it
  c before I leave the house

4 How often do you talk to your friends during lessons?
  a never   **b** sometimes   **c** always

5 Is it funny to take your friend's pencil case during the lesson?
  a Yes   **b** I don't know   **c** No

6 When do you normally arrive for your lessons?
  a when you want to
  b after the lesson starts
  c before the lesson starts

♡ Like

2 **Write a class contract.**

1 We must arrive on time.

2 _____

3 _____

4 _____

5 _____

6 When we do all these things correctly, we can:

  • _____

  • _____

Values: units 1 and 2 | social responsibility

1 Read and order the text.

	his car. Fire fighters had to cut the car door
	accident. An ambulance took Harry
	much better. He's going to leave
	had a bad car accident. His car hit a
	the hospital a team of doctors and
	officers phoned the hospital and
	Harry's life. Now, two weeks later, Harry is
	lorry and he couldn't get out of
	told the nurses about Harry and his
	which helped stop traffic. At
	to the hospital with a police car
	nurses worked together to save
1	Last week William's dad, Harry,
	hospital and go home to his family.
	and pull Harry out. Police

accident   Best wishes   great job   help
now better   operate   save life   two weeks ago

2 Write an email to thank the fire fighters.

Imagine that you are William. Write a letter to say thank you to the fire fighters, police officers and doctors who saved your dad's life. Use these words to help you.

Dear Superheroes,

Tell the truth but don't hurt

1 **Read and answer the questions.**

It's always important to tell the truth because this is the right thing to do. But sometimes the truth can hurt, and we don't want to make people feel bad or unhappy. We can still tell the truth without hurting people's feelings. We just need to choose our words very carefully and think before we speak.

1 Why is it important to tell the truth? _____

2 How can telling the truth sometimes make people feel? _____

3 How can we tell the truth without hurting people's feelings? _____

2 **Imagine a situation and write about choosing your words carefully.**

Value your friendships

 1 Write the sentences and questions.

1 I / help / can / my / friend? / How <u>How can I help my friend?</u>

2 tell / didn't / I / the / truth. _____

3 speak / should / Who / he / to? _____

4 friend / best / in / cheats / My / exams. _____

5 really / big / made / I've / mistake. / a _____

6 do? / should / I / What _____

2 Read the letter and answer the questions.

Dear Betty and Robert,

I'm worried about my friend, Deniz. He's got some new friends at school and they like doing bad things. Deniz really wants to be part of their group. They told him to go to the shopping centre and steal some things. Deniz doesn't feel that this is wrong. He has started to take little things from a small shop near home. He says he's practising because there are a lot of cameras in the big shopping centre. I told him that this group of boys aren't really his friends and that the police can catch him, but he doesn't want to listen and laughs at me. He thinks it's a joke. What should I do?

Yours,

Lucas

1 How can Lucas help Deniz? <u>He should</u> _____

2 Who can Lucas talk to? _____

3 Should Lucas tell Deniz's parents? _____

4 Should Lucas tell a teacher? _____

 3 Write a reply to Lucas.

_____

Grammar reference

1 **Write the times.**

1 **7.20** Quinn got up at <u>twenty past seven</u>.

2 **7.45** He had a shower at _____ .

3 **7.55** He got dressed at _____ .

4 **8.05** He ate his breakfast at _____ .

5 **8.25** He went to school at _____ .

6 **8.50** He arrived at school at _____ .

2 **Read and write.**

1 They're going to play tennis. (hockey)   <u>No, they aren't. They're going to play hockey.</u>

2 She's going to eat some cheese. (meat)   _____

3 He's going to have lunch at school. (home)   _____

4 We're going to get up early. (late)   _____

5 I'm going to buy a new smartphone. (comic)   _____

6 It's going to rain. (snow)

3 **Read and choose the right words.**

1 She rode her bike **(along)** / **left** the road.

2 They drove **past** / **right** the school.

3 He took the fourth street on the **straight on** / **right**.

4 The museum was **across** / **corner** the street.

5 I turned **straight on** / **left** at the post office.

6 The bus stopped at the **corner** / **across**.

4 **Read and order the words.**

1   **his**   **George wasn't**   **homework.**   **doing**
<u>George wasn't doing his homework.</u>

2   **in the**   **Sarah skiing**   **mountains?**   **Was**

3   I   bath.   having a   wasn't

_____

4   to an   sailing   island.   David was

_____

5   Emma and Harry   the park.   through   were running

_____

6   the bus stop?   Were   waiting at   you

_____

5 Answer the questions.

1 What are these bowls made of? (silver)   They're made of silver.

2 What's this comic made of? (paper)   _____

3 What are his shoes made of? (leather)   _____

4 What's her scarf made of? (wool)   _____

5 What are windows made of? (glass)   _____

6 What's that watch made of? (gold)   _____

6 Complete the sentences.

cheese   feel   It   like   ~~tired~~

1 She looked _____tired_____ .

2 They tasted _____ mangoes.

3 It smelled like _____ .

4 We didn't _____ sad.

5 _____ doesn't sound very nice.

7 Read and write 'Yes, you should.' or 'No, you shouldn't.'

1 Should you leave your rubbish on the ground?   No, you shouldn't.

2 Should you play your music very loudly?   _____

3 Should you use sun cream when you go to the beach?   _____

4 Should you play with animals in fields?   _____

5 Should you wear strong shoes when you walk in the mountains?   _____

6 Should you drink water from a river?   _____

8 Write questions and answers.

1 she / ever / climb / mountain? (✓)   Has she ever climbed a mountain?   Yes, she has.

2 they / ever / enter / competition? (✗)   _____   _____

3 he / ever / play / table tennis? (✗)   _____   _____

4 they / ever / make / snowman? (✓)   _____   _____

5 you / ever / see / the Olympics? (✗)   _____   _____

Irregular verbs

Infinitive	Past tense	Past participle
be	was / were	been
be called	was / were called	been called
be going to	was / were going to	been going to
begin	began	begun
break	broke	broken
bring	brought	brought
buy	bought	bought
can	could	–
catch	caught	caught
choose	chose	chosen
come	came	come
cut	cut	cut
do	did	done
draw	drew	drawn
drink	drank	drunk
drive	drove	driven
dry	dried	dried
eat	ate	eaten
fall	fell	fallen
fall over	fell over	fallen over
feel	felt	felt
find	found	found
find out	found out	found out
fly	flew	flown
forget	forgot	forgotten
get	got	got
get (un)dressed	got (un)dressed	got (un)dressed
get (up / on / off)	got (up / on / off)	got (up / on / off)
get to	got to	got to
give	gave	given
go	went	gone / been
go out	went out	gone / been out
go shopping	went shopping	gone / been shopping
grow	grew	grown
have	had	had
have got	had	had
have (got) to	had to	had to
hear	heard	heard
hide	hid	hidden
hit	hit	hit
hold	held	held
hurt	hurt	hurt
keep	kept	kept
know	knew	known

Infinitive	Past tense	Past participle
learn	learnt / learned	learnt / learned
leave	left	left
let	let	let
lie down	lay down	lain down
lose	lost	lost
make	made	made
make sure	made sure	made sure
mean	meant	meant
meet	met	met
must	had to	had to
put	put	put
put on	put on	put on
read	read	read
ride	rode	ridden
run	ran	run
say	said	said
see	saw	seen
sell	sold	sold
send	sent	sent
should	–	–
sing	sang	sung
sit	sat	sat
sleep	slept	slept
smell	smelt / smelled	smelt / smelled
speak	spoke	spoken
spell	spelt / spelled	spelt / spelled
spend	spent	spent
stand	stood	stood
steal	stole	stolen
swim	swam	swum
swing	swung	swung
take	took	taken
take a photo / picture	took a photo / picture	taken a photo / picture
take off	took off	taken off
teach	taught	taught
tell	told	told
think	thought	thought
throw	threw	thrown
understand	understood	understood
wake up	woke up	woken up
wear	wore	worn
win	won	won
write	wrote	written